Bliss on Toast

Prue Leith

Prue Leith

Bliss
on
Toast

75 Simple Recipes

BLOOMSBURY PUBLISHING
LONDON · OXFORD · NEW YORK · NEW DELHI · SYDNEY

BLOOMSBURY PUBLISHING

Bloomsbury Publishing Plc

50 Bedford Square, London, WC1B 3DP, UK

29 Earlsfort Terrace, Dublin 2, Ireland

BLOOMSBURY, BLOOMSBURY PUBLISHING and the Diana logo are
trademarks of Bloomsbury Publishing Plc

First published in Great Britain 2022

A catalogue record for this book is available from the British Library.

ISBN: HB: 978-1-5266-5423-6; eBook: 978-1-5266-5422-9;
ePDF: 978-1-5266-5421-2

2 4 6 8 10 9 7 5 3 1

Project Editor: Lucy Bannell

Designer: Evi O. Studio | Kait Polkinghorne

Photographer: Haarala Hamilton

Food Stylist: Hanna Miller / Katrina Whittaker

Food Styling Assistant: Joanna Jackson

Prop Stylist: Jennifer Kay

Indexer: Vanessa Bird

Printed and bound in China by C&C Offset Printing Co. Ltd

To find out more about our authors and books visit
www.bloomsbury.com and sign up for our newsletters.

For John, who has eaten a lot of stuff
on toast, not all of it bliss.

This little book comes out of a long habit (the 30-odd years since my children left home) of eating something on toast on Sunday nights in front of the telly. The simplest of old favourites – such as variations on baked beans on toast, scrambles on toast, mushrooms on toast – are here for their wonderfully comforting vibe. But then, during the Covid pandemic, I started to experiment with more sophisticated combinations which make cooking for two original, and, importantly, good looking. They are still easy though.

For 18 months I did a column for *The Oldie* magazine, producing one 'Bliss on Toast' each month. The recipes just consisted of a title, say 'Fried Pineapple on Brioche with Ice Cream', with a picture. I enlisted the help of my friend, Katrina Whittaker (aka the chef Miss Ingredient) who cooked and photographed the recipes. All the reader had to do was follow the picture. I'd like to think that most home cooks will be able to do the same from the photographs in this book. Or at least get inspiration from them and make something similar. But I know that many people are beginner or nervous cooks, so I have also included a proper recipe for each.

I've never understood the kitchen purist's objections to ready-made sauces, or food from packets and cans. The great French chef Escoffier put canned tomatoes and bottled white asparagus on the map. My first husband would happily have lived on canned sardines. What matters is the quality. Escoffier's large white asparagus are a treat; most green asparagus in cans is mushy and only good for soup. A good brand of baked beans can be rich and flavourful; a cheap one watery and tasteless. I almost never take the time to bash the tough stalks of lemon grass into submission. Why would I when great lemon grass paste can be had in a tube? Because speed and convenience are important to today's home cooks, I've gone for bottled, canned and ready-prepped ingredients where I can. But, on the Keen Cooks pages, I've included tips on how to make things at home too. There's a flatbread recipe which is foolproof and fast to make, for instance, certainly faster than going to the supermarket to buy it. On the other hand, a packet of ready-made flatbreads from one's freezer is even quicker.

I have recommended suitable breads for the recipes, but of course they are widely interchangeable. I tend to buy the same wholemeal sourdough for weeks, and then suddenly get tired of it and focaccia will have a run, or a fat white bloomer, or light rye. I'm not expecting anyone to follow the recipes exactly. For example, I have occasionally suggested ingredients which are unlikely to be in the store cupboard or are only available online. They are never essential, but I'm hoping some of the recipes will inspire readers to have a go at something different.

Writing, testing and – most of all – consuming these Bliss on Toasts has been a huge pleasure. I hope reading, making and eating them will be for you too. Let me know on social media, or see www.prue-leith.com.

Ⓥ = vegan

All recipes serve 2

🐦 **@prueleith**

📷 **@prueleith or @miss.ingredient**

ⓕ **prueleithofficial**

Cheese
& Eggs

Camembert & blackberries with chilli sauce on rye

Early autumn brings fat little brambles in the hedgerows. In the far-off days when I had time to go brambling with the children, wild blackberries would have adorned this treat. Now I'm lazier, and busier, it's more likely to be monster ones from the supermarket.

2 slices of rye bread

butter for spreading (optional)

100g ripe Camembert cheese

2 tsp sweet chilli sauce

handful of blackberries, halved if you like

handful of rocket

Toast the bread. Spread it with butter, if you like.

Slice the cheese and arrange it as best you can on the toast, then drizzle over the chilli sauce, sprinkle with blackberries and top with rocket.

TIP
If the Camembert isn't ripe enough, warm it a bit (in 10-second bursts) in the microwave.

Welsh rarebit with crisp bacon on granary

This has got to be the most popular Bliss on Toast in my family. Who doesn't like a toastie? Especially if the cheese is a true Welsh rarebit rather than just a slice of processed stuff. I like the bacon in long streaky strips, but scrunched-up bacon bits are fine too.

4 rindless streaky bacon rashers, or pancetta slices

1 tbsp oil for frying

1 heaped tsp butter

1 heaped tsp plain flour

4 tbsp milk

80g mature Cheddar cheese, grated

1 tsp Dijon mustard

2 thick slices of granary bread

Start by frying the bacon slowly in the oil until crisp, curly and brown. Drain on a piece of kitchen paper.

Use the same pan to make the rarebit sauce: melt the butter, stir in the flour, add the milk, then bring to the boil, stirring. Add the cheese and mustard and mix well. Take off the heat while you toast the bread. Don't worry if all the cheese is not melted.

When ready to serve, preheat the grill to maximum, spread the cheese mix on the toasts, then put them under the grill until bubbling and brown. Add the bacon and serve.

TIP
This cheesy mix, spread thinly on thinner toast and cut into small squares, is a perfect snack with drinks.

Spicy ezme salad with fried egg on country loaf

This is a brilliant and unusual light lunch. The Turkish salad should be cold and the fried egg hot: a surprising and delicious combo. The combination of temperatures in the mouth is very good. By 'country loaf' I mean any homemade or artisan bread, the rougher the better.

2 medium-thick slices
of country loaf

2 eggs

oil for frying

1 tbsp pomegranate seeds

For the salad

1 small onion,
finely chopped

good pinch of ground sumac

½ red pepper, deseeded
and finely chopped

¼ cucumber, skin on,
finely chopped

pinch of chilli flakes

1 tbsp olive oil

1 tsp wine vinegar

1 tsp pomegranate molasses

salt and freshly ground
black pepper

Toast the bread and put each slice on a good-sized plate.

Put the onion and sumac into a big bowl and use the end of a rolling pin to crush them together until the onion is pink. Then add the rest of the salad ingredients, season to taste and mix well. Pile the salad on top of the toast and set aside while you deal with the eggs.

When ready to serve, fry the eggs in a little oil until the whites are set but the yolks still runny. Slide the eggs on to the salad and sprinkle with the pomegranate seeds and a bit more pepper.

TIPS

- If you haven't any (or can't get) pomegranate molasses, date syrup or balsamic glaze make good substitutes. Or even a combination of Worcestershire sauce and redcurrant jelly. Basically, you want a sauce that is both sweet and interesting.

- Sumac is, for me, the defining taste of Turkey, and is a useful zesty spice to have. Great with feta cheese, on baked potatoes, in salads, or to liven up a stew or soup.

- You can omit or go easy on the chilli, or double up on it. I like enough to notice but not so much that the salad's flavour is obliterated.

Tenderstem broccoli & egg with romesco on sourdough

It's worth making romesco sauce to go with anything grilled. The broccoli can be steamed or boiled of course, but it's more of a treat if fried.

I'm often asked for a definitive method of poaching eggs, and I have to say the main secret is freshness. If an egg is very fresh the white will be thick and viscous and cling to the yolk. If it is stale, it will be watery and thin and flow all over the pan. For an alternative way to poach eggs, see page 24.

2 large slices of sourdough bread

butter for frying

150g Tenderstem broccoli

2 large very fresh eggs

For the romesco

½ jar roasted red peppers, drained

3 sundried tomatoes

2 tbsp flaked almonds, toasted (see tip, below)

1 large garlic clove, crushed

50ml olive oil

salt and freshly ground black pepper

Blitz together all the romesco ingredients and season with salt and pepper.

Fry the bread in a little butter to brown it on both sides. Put the fried bread on hot plates.

Lay the broccoli in the frying pan with a little more butter and fry over a medium heat, turning over when one side is brown, to brown the other.

Poach the eggs: heat a pan of water to simmering point. Use the handle of a wooden spoon to swirl it into a whirlpool. Gently crack an egg into the centre. With luck, the white will swirl round the yolk. After 3 minutes, use a slotted spoon to lift the egg on to a clean tea towel where it can be cosily covered while you poach the second.

Warm the romesco in a microwave, then spread it on the fried bread. Divide the broccoli between the slices, then put a poached egg on top of each and sprinkle with pepper.

TIP

To toast almonds, shake them in a dry pan over heat until pale brown, or cook in a microwave for 3 minutes, stirring them gently halfway.

Summer peas & beans with ricotta on sourdough

Few flavours delight and excite like the first fresh peas, mangetout and baby broad beans of summer. But hardly any of us have access to fresh peas and beans, or the time to deal with them. I confess to keeping a few packets of mixed peas, broad beans and edamame (baby soy beans) in the freezer.

100g shelled broad beans

100g shelled peas

handful of mangetout, stalks removed

1 tbsp olive oil

1 tsp balsamic glaze

1 tbsp chopped mint leaves, plus a couple of mint sprigs

50ml double cream

100g ricotta cheese

2 slices of sourdough bread, preferably seeded

butter for spreading

sea salt flakes and freshly ground black pepper

Bring a pan of water to the boil and drop in the beans. After 2 minutes, add the peas and mangetout, then boil for a further 2 minutes. Drain them and rinse briefly under the cold tap to prevent the loss of the bright green colour. (If the broad beans are large, see tip, below.) Tumble them into a bowl.

Add the olive oil, balsamic glaze and chopped mint to the peas and beans, with a pinch of sea salt and a few turns of the pepper mill.

Mix the cream and ricotta together and beat until smooth. Season lightly with salt and pepper.

Toast the bread and butter it. Spread on the ricotta and pile on the peas and beans. Add the mint sprigs to serve.

TIP
If using mature broad beans, it's worth removing their tough skins when they are cooked. Split their skins with your thumbnail, then squeeze to pop the beans out.

Figs, blue cheese, thyme & honey on bloomer

We used to have long green figs growing in my childhood garden in South Africa. They'd split a bit when ripe and we'd eat them straight from the tree, dripping with their figgy honey. In England we mostly have brown Turkey figs, which can either be wonderful or totally tasteless and dry. It's a toss-up, but I can never resist buying them. And if paired with blue cheese and a drizzle of really good honey, they are a treat. Expensive, but worth it.

3 ripe figs

150g mild blue cheese
(see tip, below)

2 slices of white bloomer

olive oil for brushing

runny honey

1 tsp thyme leaves,
stalks removed

sea salt flakes and freshly
ground black pepper

Slice the figs into slim wedges and mash the blue cheese.

Brush the bread slices on both sides with the olive oil and then toast them, or brown them on both sides in a hot frying pan.

When the toasts are cool, top them with the cheese and figs.

Sprinkle with sea salt and a few twists of the pepper mill. Drizzle a little honey over the top and sprinkle on the thyme leaves.

TIP

Any blue cheese will be good. I like a creamy, fairly mild Gorgonzola or Cotswold Blue, but if you like a sharper cheese, Roquefort or Stilton will fit the bill.

Poached eggs, rose harissa butter on granary toast

This recipe is a whole new take on poached eggs on toast, especially beloved of chilli lovers. I'd never heard of harissa five years ago, yet now I'd hate to live without it. It's a North African chilli paste, made milder, more interesting, fragrant and delicious by the addition of herbs and spices and – in the case of rose harissa – of rose petals.

2 large slices of granary bread

40g soft butter

1 heaped tsp rose harissa paste

handful of rocket

4 small, very fresh eggs

sea salt flakes and freshly ground black pepper

Toast the bread.

Beat the butter with the harissa paste and spread it on the toast.

Cover with a good layer of rocket.

Poach the eggs for 3 minutes in simmering water (see page 18, or tip, below), drain and carefully place on top of the rocket. Season with salt and pepper.

TIPS

- For poaching eggs, see page 18. Or simply crack the eggs gently into almost-still simmering water in a frying pan. Use a fish slice to carefully ensure the eggs do not stick to the bottom. When poached, lift them out on a slotted spoon so that they will drain. You can help them dry by holding the spoon on a folded tea towel and dabbing the egg gently with the sides of the towel, then tip them, one by one, on to the toast.

- If an egg sinks in a glass of cold water, it's fresh. If it bobs to the top, it's less fresh: it has developed an air pocket, which happens over time. Less than fresh eggs are impossible to poach, as the whites disperse in the water.

Duck egg, rainbow chard with Dijon butter on granary

Fried or poached eggs on spinach (*oeufs Florentine*, for example) are classic. But other leafy greens work well too: chard, kale, chopped sprouts, or a mix of any cooked, buttered green veg. Best of all are wild garlic leaves (see tip, below).

Duck's eggs have a slightly different texture from hen's eggs, but taste much the same. They are bigger though. If using hen's eggs, I'd suggest two per person.

2 large slices of granary bread

60g soft butter

1 heaped tsp Dijon mustard

6 rainbow chard leaves (or see tip, below)

1 garlic clove, crushed

2 very fresh duck eggs

sea salt flakes and freshly ground black pepper

Toast the bread.

Beat half the butter with all the Dijon mustard and spread it on the toasts.

Cut the stalks from the chard leaves. Slice the stalks, discarding any tough ends. Bring a pan of water to the boil and add the sliced stalks, then 2 minutes later the leaves. Boil for a further 2 minutes, then drain and dry gently but thoroughly on a tea towel. Spread the chard on the buttered mustardy toasts.

Melt the rest of the butter in a frying pan and fry the garlic very briefly – just until you can smell it – then crack in the duck eggs and cook slowly until the whites are set and the yolks still runny. Lift on to the buttered toasts, tip over any garlicky butter from the pan and sprinkle with salt and pepper.

TIP

Wild garlic is even better for this dish than chard, but it is only very briefly in season in early spring and not that easy to get hold of even then. If you are lucky enough to find some, you can omit the garlic clove in this recipe. If picking wild garlic, make sure you do it when the leaves are young and the plants have not yet flowered. Once in bloom, the leaves – to my mind – are too strong.

Bubble & squeak with hollandaise on fried bread

This is the gourmet version of bubble and squeak. Very rich and fattening, but irresistible. You can buy hollandaise sauce in a jar; it's not exactly like the real thing, but it's good all the same.

2 streaky bacon rashers

dripping, oil, or butter for frying

140g boiled and mashed potato (leftover is fine)

handful of cooked cabbage, or any leftover green vegetables, roughly chopped

2 thick slices of white bread

2–3 tbsp store-bought hollandaise sauce (or see tip, below)

a little milk, if needed

salt and freshly ground black pepper

Fry the bacon in a little fat until it is crisp all over. Lift out the rashers, allow to cool, then chop them up.

Mix the potato, green vegetables and bacon bits together. Taste the mixture and add salt and pepper as necessary. Shape into 2 patties each about 2.5cm thick.

Fry the slices of bread on both sides in the bacon pan, adding a little more fat if needed, then put them on separate warm plates. In the same pan, fry the potato patties gently to brown both sides and heat through. Put them on top of the bread.

Spoon over the hollandaise sauce. (You may need to thin it with a little milk to get it to a just-pouring consistency.) Grind a little pepper on top.

TIP

If you'd like to make your own hollandaise, there are instructions for 2 methods (by hand and with a blender) in the Keen Cooks section (see page 174).

Scrambles with fried prosciutto on sourdough

This is a mighty popular Sunday night supper in our house. It's a bit extravagant to go frying prosciutto but it gets wonderfully crisp all over, so I think it's worth it. I like my scrambles with a good handful of chopped parsley too, though some people consider this sacrilege.

My husband likes Marmite on the toast under his scrambles. Each to his own. I wouldn't advise Marmite, prosciutto *and* parsley.

butter for spreading and frying

2 slices of sourdough bread, toasted

4 slices of prosciutto

oil for frying

5 eggs

dash of milk

1 tbsp chopped parsley leaves

salt and freshly ground black pepper

Butter the pieces of toast and put them ready on warm plates.

Fry the prosciutto in 2 tsp oil until it shrinks and the colour darkens. Lift out and drain on kitchen paper. The prosciutto slices will crisp up as they cool a little.

Whisk the eggs with 2 tbsp or so of milk and season with salt and pepper. Melt a little more butter in the frying pan and pour in the eggs. Keep stirring with a spatula as the eggs thicken. Take the pan off the heat before the eggs have quite set and tip them on to the toast. Add the crisp prosciutto.

Sprinkle heavily with the parsley.

TIP

This quick method of scrambling eggs gives an almost omelette-like texture, which I like. Albert Roux, the great Michelin-starred chef, insisted that the only correct way was to cook them slowly in a double boiler or in a bowl over simmering water, stirring all the time. It produces rather more liquid eggs, like a thick sauce. Takes ages though.

Mozzarella in carrozza

'Mozzarella in a carriage' is not strictly 'on toast'. It is bliss though – the most indulgent, satisfying, delicious combination of fried bread and melting cheese you can imagine. It's just a fried cheese sarnie really, but what could be better than that? It is a bit messy to make and messy to eat, but absolutely worth every calorie... and there are plenty of those!

4 slices of ordinary supermarket white bread from a large loaf

75g mozzarella cheese, sliced

4 basil leaves

75ml milk

2 tbsp plain flour

1 large egg, lightly beaten

olive oil for frying

salt and freshly ground black pepper

Carefully cut the crusts off the bread and make 2 big square sandwiches with the cheese, seasoning them with salt and pepper and adding 2 basil leaves to each as you go. Make sure you leave a bit of a margin free from cheese round the edge so you can press the edges together. (Fresh, soft commercial bread is so squishy that it is easy to make a good seal.)

Put the milk, flour and egg into separate shallow bowls or plates with a lip. Lay the sandwiches briefly on each side in the milk, then dip the edges in the flour (you are trying to ensure a good seal) and finally turn the whole sandwich carefully in the egg.

Heat a couple of tbsp oil in a frying pan over a medium-low heat and fry the sandwiches to brown them on both sides. Drain them on kitchen paper. Yum.

TIPS

- You can make all sorts of versions of this: try adding tomato sauce (for homemade, see page 174), olives, onion marmalade or chutney to the filling. And almost any cheese works. Cheddar makes a great fried cheese toastie, but it doesn't produce the lovely stretchy strings that mozzarella does.

- Using a pastry cutter, you can make small round *carrozza* for snacks to have with drinks.

Goat's cheese, spinach & red onion on seeded brown

In the 1990s, grilled goat's cheese was all the rage, usually eaten with salad as a starter, or as a veggie main course. We served it at my restaurant on toast with chilli jam and grapes, and very good it was too. Maybe it's time for a revival. I like the slightly crumbly, soft Italian cheese that comes in large logs.

2 slices of seeded
brown bread

butter for spreading

1 tbsp red onion marmalade

handful of baby
spinach leaves

2 fat slices of goat's cheese
from a large log (see
tip, below)

Toast the bread, butter it, then spread with the red onion marmalade and top with the baby spinach leaves.

Preheat the grill to maximum and grill the cheese slices on a lined baking sheet as close to the grill as you dare – you want to brown the top before the cheese melts too much. Use a fish slice to carefully transfer the slices to the spinach-covered toasts.

TIPS

- Goat's cheese is inclined to crumble as you slice it. If you heat a knife blade in boiling water for 20 seconds, then dry it before slicing, you will get intact slices.

- If the goat's cheese is fresh, the downy white skin will be delicious. But if it has become at all discoloured or wet, cut it off.

Kale, chilli, burrata & tapenade on sourdough

You can buy mozzarella almost anywhere but its more luxurious cousin, burrata, is still something of a rarity other than in the largest of supermarkets and the best delis. Burrata is basically mozzarella stuffed with cream: decadent in the extreme, and all the better for that. I like to eat this while the kale is still hot, as I like the contrast with the cold creamy burrata.

large handful of roughly chopped curly kale leaves

½ red chilli, finely chopped

1 garlic clove, crushed

extra virgin olive oil

2–3 tbsp water

2 slices of sourdough bread

2 tsp black olive tapenade

1 burrata, drained of whey

½ tsp coriander seeds, toasted and slightly crushed (see page 40)

sea salt flakes

Put the kale, chilli, garlic, 1 tbsp olive oil and all the measured water into a wok or frying pan and stir-fry for 4–5 minutes until the water has evaporated and the kale is bright green and beginning to crisp up round the edges. Take off the heat.

Toast the bread slices, spread thinly with the tapenade and drizzle a little olive oil over them. Put them on plates and arrange the kale on top.

Divide the burrata into 4 and put 2 pieces on top of each kale-covered toast. Sprinkle with the coriander seeds and a pinch of salt.

TIPS

- There is more power in the seeds of chilli than in the flesh. So if you don't like it too hot, deseed the chilli before chopping.

- Kale with chilli and garlic makes really good crisps. Instead of stir-frying them, mix the kale leaves (which must be dry) thoroughly with the chilli, garlic and a little olive oil. Spread out in a single sparse layer on a baking sheet and cook in an oven preheated to 150°C/fan 130°C/Gas Mark 2 for 20 minutes, until dried out and crisped up.

Fried halloumi in pitta pockets

I never thought much of halloumi until, when I was a judge on *My Kitchen Rules,* one of our contestants was a young Syrian woman who had fled Aleppo with her family. They'd been well-off at home, having a good life in a city they loved. But, as refugees in the UK, they struggled to find work and she turned to her skills as a home cook to try to make some money. She made halloumi in her kitchen and sold it to the other mums at the school gates. It was sensationally good.

1 pack of halloumi cheese

1 tbsp plain flour

2 tbsp olive oil for frying

1 tbsp capers

1 tbsp chopped parsley leaves

juice of 1 small lemon

1 garlic clove, crushed

2 pitta breads

freshly ground black pepper

Cut the halloumi into thick even sticks and toss them on a plate in the flour mixed with 3 turns of the pepper mill.

Fry the sticks over a medium heat in the oil, turning them to get them golden all over.

Mix the capers, parsley, lemon juice and garlic together.

Warm the pittas briefly in a microwave or a dry frying pan, then open up the side of each to form a wide pocket.

Drop the fried sticks of halloumi into the pockets and then drizzle the herby dressing in, on top of the cheese.

TIP

Pitta bread is best eaten warm. If the breads have been allowed to cool, they can be reheated successfully in a frying pan.

Goat's cheese, pear & balsamic on baguette

I first had these as a canapé at a drinks party, made from a French *ficelle* (a long skinny version of a baguette), the thin ends of Conference pears and small rounds of a French goat's cheese. I couldn't believe that in 50 years of cooking and catering I'd never thought of anything so simple and perfect. As *ficelle* is impossible to find, my recipe here is for a supper dish of a larger version. The size is dictated by the diameter of cheese and baguette and if, as here, you only have a thin baguette, you might need three toasts per person, and a good bit of salad. To slice goat's cheese without it crumbling, see the tip on page 35.

6 thin slices cut from the middle of a baguette

½ tsp coriander seeds

2 ripe Conference pears

6 thin slices of goat's cheese

balsamic glaze for drizzling

a few basil leaves, shredded

Toast the baguette slices lightly, then lay them on a grill tray. Preheat the grill to maximum and let it get blazing hot.

Put the coriander seeds into a small pan and shake them over a medium heat until they smell fragrant and are darkening slightly. Tip on to a saucer to stop them overcooking. Crush them slightly with the end of a rolling pin.

Cut 6 slices of pear roughly the diameter of the bread (you may need more if you have skinny pears). Don't worry about any core in the slices.

Top each toast with a slice of pear, then a slice of cheese. Drizzle a little balsamic glaze on each. Grill until the cheese is starting to melt. Sprinkle with the basil and coriander seeds. Eat warm.

TIP

I find the best cheese for this is Italian, sold wholesale in 1kg logs. Many delis sell it by weight, but I buy them whole. They keep for weeks in the fridge in their cardboard box, or a beeswax wrap.

Vegetarian
& Vegan

Tomatoes with English pesto on toasted focaccia

I think I prefer this English version of pesto even to the classic Italian basil one. It's lighter and more versatile. It's good with pasta, on pizza, or just as flavouring for salad dressing, or indeed to serve with grilled chicken or lamb chops. Just about anything really!

2 squares of focaccia

4–6 big slices of ripe tomato

For the pesto

20g walnuts

30g bunch of parsley

1 garlic clove, crushed

30g Cheddar cheese, finely grated

75ml rapeseed oil

salt and freshly ground black pepper

Preheat the oven to 200°C/Fan 180°C/Gas Mark 6. Put the walnuts on a baking tray and into the hot oven for 5 minutes to toast. Or toast them in the microwave for 5 minutes, giving them a stir halfway through.

Chop the stalks of the parsley, which have a lot of flavour you don't want to waste, with a sharp knife. (Chopping in the machine can result in stringy bits – better to start by hand.) Put them, the parsley leaves and garlic into a blender and chop briefly. Then add the Cheddar and walnuts and blend again. At this point you will need to add the oil to loosen the paste. When everything is in, blitz to a smooth-ish sauce and season with salt and pepper.

Toast or grill the focaccia pieces to warm them through, then spread with the pesto and overlap the tomato slices on top.

TIPS

The pesto will keep for a couple of weeks in the fridge if stored in a jar with a little more oil on top to keep the air out. But it will lose its brilliant colour, sadly.

(v) To make it vegan, use vegan Cheddar or any other hard vegan cheese.

Roast butternut with pear on toasted oat & barley bread

(V)

The taste of butternut squash takes me right back to my childhood in South Africa. They used to grow on our compost heap, competing with pumpkins and courgettes. We generally had them mashed as a veg or puréed into a soup. The idea of serving squash on toast was unheard of.

200g pumpkin, or butternut squash

2–3 tbsp olive oil

a few sage leaves

½ small ripe pear, cored

2 slices of oat and barley country loaf, or similar

sea salt flakes and freshly ground black pepper

Preheat the oven to 180°C/fan 160°C/Gas Mark 4.

Peel the pumpkin or squash, remove the seeds and cut the flesh into bite-sized chunks. Turn them in the oil, then spread them out on a baking sheet. Add the sage leaves and roast in the hot oven.

The sage leaves will be crisp after about 10 minutes. When they are, remove them and continue cooking the squash for another 20 minutes or so until soft.

Meanwhile slice the pear, with or without the skin as you prefer.

Toast the bread and pile the hot squash and the raw pear on top. Finish with salt, pepper and the sage leaves.

TIP

If the pumpkin or squash is freshly picked and young, the skin will not be too hard and you need not peel it, as it will soften on cooking. Sadly, as the squash ages (and many keep for months, even unrefrigerated), it gets tough and peeling with a large sharp knife or a very robust vegetable peeler is necessary.

Grilled courgettes with cashew pesto on rye

It's amazing how grilling, griddling or frying enhances the taste of courgette, concentrating its flavour. I use a ridged griddle pan with a little olive oil. Cashews make a slightly lighter and creamier pesto than pine nuts.

2 medium courgettes

olive oil for brushing

2 big slices of light rye bread

For the pesto

20g cashew nuts

1 garlic clove, crushed

30g Parmesan cheese, finely grated

handful of basil leaves

75ml olive oil

salt and freshly ground black pepper

First make the pesto. Put the nuts and garlic in a food processor or blender and blitz. Then add the rest of the ingredients with a pinch each of salt and pepper and process until smooth.

Now for the courgettes: cut them lengthways into 3–4 slices each. Turn them in olive oil.

If you have a ridged pan or sandwich maker, all the better, but stripes aren't essential. A good frying pan will do fine. Cook the slices until brown and floppy (which means they are cooked through).

Toast the bread and put it on warm plates. Pile on the courgettes and dot with the pesto.

TIPS

You will have too much pesto I'm afraid, but it's hard to make smaller quantities in a blender. It will keep for a week or so in the fridge and will be good on pasta, in risotto, on grilled chicken or lamb, or will liven up a vegetable soup. You can freeze it too.

(v) To make it vegan, use vegan Parmesan.

Balsamic aubergines with pumpkin seeds on chilli bread

Fried aubergine slices make a really satisfying veggie dish. They are usually served spread with tomato purée and topped with melted cheese, but I prefer them like this: lots of garlic in the mayo and chilli in the bread. No chilli bread? Never mind, just add some chilli with the garlic.

2 tsp pumpkin seeds

1 medium aubergine

about 2 tbsp balsamic glaze

2 tbsp olive oil, plus more for the pan

2 tbsp mayonnaise

1 tbsp tomato purée

2 garlic cloves, crushed

½ red chilli, finely chopped, or a pinch of chilli flakes (optional)

2 good slices of chilli bread (or see recipe introduction)

1 tbsp oregano leaves

sea salt flakes and freshly ground black pepper

Toast the pumpkin seeds in a dry frying pan, keeping them moving. They will puff up and pop. Tip them on to a cold saucer.

Slice the aubergine into 6 thick slices.

Whisk the balsamic glaze and oil together in a bowl and turn the aubergine in this mix. Leave for 10 minutes while you oil and heat a ridged griddle pan. When good and hot, cook the aubergine slices until brown on the undersides and soft right through. Don't worry about browning the second sides.

Mix the mayonnaise with the tomato purée, garlic and chilli (if using).

Toast the bread and spread thickly with the mayo. Sprinkle with half the oregano. Cover with the warm aubergine slices, browned sides up, season with salt and pepper and sprinkle heavily with the pumpkin seeds and the rest of the oregano.

TIPS

- You can grill the aubergine or fry it in an ordinary frying pan. But if you have a ridged griddle pan or sandwich toaster you'll get the fancy stripes.
- Use soy sauce if you don't have balsamic glaze.
- (V) To make it vegan, use vegan mayo.

Falafel, edamame & red pepper hummus on flatbread

Ready-made falafel can be delicious (M&S do a good one) though, let's face it, they can be pretty boring. But even dull ones can by enlivened by fresh herbs, a good red pepper hummus and really garlicky yogurt. Flatbreads are sold in most supermarkets, but are a doddle to make too. There's a recipe in the Keen Cooks section (see page 178).

1 garlic clove, crushed

100g plain yogurt

50g shelled edamame beans

single-portion pack of ready-made falafel

2 tbsp red pepper hummus (for homemade, see page 176)

2 small fresh round flatbreads

1 tbsp chopped mint leaves

pinch of sea salt flakes and freshly ground black pepper

Crush the garlic with the salt (see tip, below). Mix the yogurt with the crushed garlic.

Boil the beans for 3 minutes, drain and rinse briefly with cold water, then drain again.

Break the falafel into rough chunks.

Spread the hummus on the flatbreads. Add the falafel and beans and top with the yogurt. Sprinkle on the mint and some black pepper to serve.

TIPS

- If serving this hot, I like to warm the flatbreads briefly in the oven. If it is for a picnic or lunchbox, large flat wraps (cold) would be better than round flatbreads. Roll the filling up tightly in the wraps and parcel up in greaseproof paper.

- To remove the skin of garlic, cut off and discard both ends of the garlic clove. Bash the clove with something flat and heavy such as the base of a jam jar. This will split the papery skin and make it easy to slip off. To crush garlic without a crusher: on a board, cut the peeled clove into the smallest bits you can, then add a good pinch of salt and crush the salt and garlic to a paste with the flat of a round-bladed knife.

- (v) To make it vegan, use vegan flatbreads and unsweetened smooth coconut yogurt.

Avocado, summer tomatoes & tapenade on olive bread

(v)

Fresh salad-y things on toast work well if bound with a good-tasting olive oil, or something rich like a tapenade or aïoli. But you do need deep-flavoured veg: vine-ripened tomatoes, ripe avocados, fresh rocket. The date syrup isn't strictly necessary, but its sweetness makes a nice contrast with salty tapenade.

When I was at chef school we were taught to always skin tomatoes (by dunking them in boiling water for 10 seconds to loosen the skins) and then remove the seeds, but I seldom bother now. It seems a waste and I really like the tomato juice (you lose most of that if you remove the seeds) softening the fried bread a bit.

2 slices of olive sourdough bread

extra virgin olive oil

100g flavourful small tomatoes, preferably multicoloured

1 large ripe avocado

2 tbsp tapenade

a few basil sprigs, or a handful of rocket

date syrup for drizzling

salt and freshly ground black pepper

Cut the sourdough into long thick slices.

Pour a little olive oil into a frying pan, or brush a ridged griddle pan with it. Heat the pan, then cook the bread slices on both sides until brown, adding more oil for the second side.

While they are frying, cut the tomatoes and avocado into small chunks. Mix them together and season lightly with salt and pepper.

When the bread is done, spread it with the tapenade, then pile on the avocado and tomatoes and top with basil or rocket. Pour a thin squiggle of date syrup over each one.

TIPS

- Avocado slices or chunks will refrain from discolouring for hours if rinsed in cold water.
- Multicoloured 'heritage' tomatoes are generally a good bet. Available only in summer, they are usually vine-ripened and delicious and are a mix of yellow, red, green and purple.

Grilled aubergines with smoked cheese on toasted baguette

This is almost my favourite lunch. Aubergine needs slight charring to bring out its flavour. If using tomato ketchup instead of a tomato sauce, go easy – it's a very overpowering flavour.

1 aubergine

olive oil for cooking

18cm piece from the middle of a baguette

1 large garlic clove, crushed

100ml bottled tomato sauce (see tip, below)

50g smoked cheese, grated

a few basil leaves

sea salt flakes and freshly ground black pepper

Preheat the grill to maximum. Cut the aubergine lengthways into 10 thin slices. Brush the slices with olive oil and grill on one side only until brown.

Split the length of baguette in half and toast or grill the pieces.

In a small pan, cook the garlic briefly in 1 tsp olive oil, then add the tomato sauce and warm through.

Arrange the aubergine slices on the baguette pieces, spoon on the tomato sauce and top with the grated cheese.

Put back under the grill or into a hot oven (preheated to 200°C/fan 180°C/Gas Mark 6) to melt the cheese. Sprinkle with salt, pepper and basil leaves.

TIPS

Tomato sauce is easy to make. See the Keen Cooks section, page 174.

(V) To make it vegan, use vegan smoked cheese.

Jersey Royals, nasturtium & garlic mayo on oat bread

Carbs on carbs? I know, it sounds excessive, but Jersey Royals (or your own new potatoes just dug out of the garden) are so special, you *have* to break the rules. This recipe is best with freshly boiled or steamed warm spuds and any fresh herbs you like. If you grow nasturtiums, you probably know that the very young leaves are delicious – peppery and tart. But I've never seen them sold commercially, and other herbs will do as well.

handful of small nasturtium leaves

4 tbsp mayonnaise

1 small garlic clove, crushed

2 slices of oat bread, toasted

5–6 Jersey Royal potatoes, freshly boiled

¼ red onion, finely sliced

1 tbsp capers, rinsed and dried (or see tip, below)

sea salt flakes and freshly ground black pepper

Shred the nasturtium leaves, keeping some for decoration. Mix the rest with the mayonnaise and garlic. Spread this on the toast.

Slice the potatoes and put them on top.

Top with the onion slices, capers and whole nasturtium leaves, scatter with a pinch of salt and pepper and serve.

TIPS

- If the potatoes have been cooked and refrigerated for a day or so, they may taste a touch 'fridgey'. My answer would be to fry them in a little butter or olive oil to gently brown them.
- I like soft oat bread, but of course any bread you prefer would be fine.
- If you do grow nasturtiums, you might like to pickle their seedpods; there's a recipe in the Keen Cooks section (see page 175). I sometimes prefer them to capers.
- (V) To make it vegan, use vegan mayo.

Tomatoes, shallots & oregano on black olive toast

(V)

It might take an hour to cook shallots down to an irresistible sweet and slightly sticky stage, but it's worth it. Of course, you could use any shallot or onion, but banana shallots are particularly sweet and retain their shape.

6 banana shallots, peeled and halved lengthways

olive oil for cooking

2 tsp brown sugar

3 vine tomatoes, halved through their equators

1 tsp thyme leaves

4 slices of black olive bread

1 large garlic clove, peeled

1 tbsp oregano leaves

sea salt flakes and freshly ground black pepper

Preheat the oven to 160°C/fan 140°C/Gas Mark 3.

Put the shallots on one side of a lined oven tray, brush generously with oil and sprinkle with the sugar. Put the tomatoes, cut sides up, on the other side of the tray, brush with more oil and sprinkle with the thyme.

Roast in the slow oven for 1 hour or until everything is very soft and beginning to caramelise.

Meanwhile, brush the bread slices on both sides with olive oil, then brown them in a hot frying pan, turning them to toast both sides. When cool enough to handle, cut the very end off the garlic clove and rub the cut end carefully all over one side of the pieces of toast.

Arrange the tomatoes and shallots on the toasts, season with salt and pepper, then top with the oregano leaves.

TIP
If you use cherry tomatoes, you'll need a handful; don't halve them, and give them only 30 minutes or so in the oven.

Mushrooms, parsley & cream on seeded brown toast

All mushrooms, wild or cultivated, common or exotic, are good like this. But I think I like the big black open supermarket mushrooms best. They make the most satisfying, comforting supper on a chilly evening, as good as boiled eggs and soldiers. The truffle oil is not necessary, but it does add another layer of decadent flavour. Don't overdo it though, it can be overpowering.

2 tbsp oil for frying

4–6 large open mushrooms, sliced

1 large garlic clove, crushed

a few drops of truffle oil

100ml single cream

2 thick slices of seeded granary or wholemeal bread

butter for spreading

1 tbsp chopped parsley leaves

salt and freshly ground black pepper

Heat the oil in a frying pan and fry the mushrooms fast enough to brown as well as cook them. Keep them moving until they are almost done, then add the garlic and fry for a minute more.

When soft and cooked, add the truffle oil and the cream to the pan, season well with salt and pepper and boil up, stirring to incorporate any mushroom residue.

Toast the bread slices, butter them and put on warm plates.

Divide the mushrooms between the slices and sprinkle heavily with parsley.

(V) To make it vegan, use vegan butter and cream.

Red pepper hummus, avocado & zhoug on rye

(V)

You can buy Yemeni zhoug sauce or paste in jars, online or from a good deli, or you can make it very quickly, as here. You can also buy red pepper hummus in most supermarkets and it is generally good quality. I only make it (see Keen Cooks, page 176) if I know I'll need a lot. If, as here, I only need a couple of spoons, a small tub from the shop does the trick.

2 slices of light rye bread

olive oil for frying

3 tbsp red pepper hummus

1 ripe avocado, sliced

1 tsp lemon juice

sea salt flakes and freshly ground black pepper

For the zhoug

large bunch of coriander

1 large garlic clove, chopped

½ tsp ground cardamom

1 tsp ground cumin

½ tsp chilli flakes

75ml olive oil

½ tsp salt

First make the zhoug. Reserve a few coriander leaves for decoration and simply process all the rest of the ingredients together in a blender.

If you have a ridged griddle pan or sandwich maker, so much the better. If not, don't worry, an ordinary frying pan will do. Heat it well. Brush the slices of bread on both sides with olive oil and fry until nicely browned all over.

Spread the toast with the hummus, then lay the avocado slices on top and season with salt and pepper.

Take 3 tbsp of the zhoug, mix the lemon juice into it, then use it to dot the top. Sprinkle with the reserved coriander leaves.

TIP

Don't be tempted to mix lemon juice into all the zhoug. As this quantity makes more than you need here, you'll have to refrigerate the rest (which will be good on grilled fish and chicken or mixed with yogurt for a dip) and the lemon juice will discolour the zhoug in the fridge. Better to add it only when you need it.

Carrot hummus with raisin & pickle on baguette (V)

Roasting, frying or grilling root vegetables – browning them in the process – deepens their flavour, which concentrates the taste, partly because the browning caramelises their sugars. This is a great way to make a hero of the humble carrot.

250g medium carrots

100ml apple cider vinegar

1 tsp sugar

1 tbsp raisins

1 tbsp olive oil for cooking, plus more for drizzling if you like

100g shop-bought hummus (or see tip, below)

25cm piece from the middle of a baguette, split in half

1 spring onion, chopped (green part as well as white)

Preheat the oven to 160°C/fan 140°C/Gas Mark 3.

Use a potato peeler to first peel and then slice 1 carrot into thin ribbons.

In a small saucepan, bring the vinegar and sugar to the boil, then take off the heat and drop the ribboned carrot and the raisins into it.

Peel the rest of the carrots and split them down the middle. Slice them on an angle into 2cm pieces, then turn in 1 tbsp olive oil. Then slow-roast them in the oven, turning them frequently, until they are soft and a bit brown, about 1 hour.

Take them out of the oven. Reserve a few good-looking carrot pieces for the top and process the rest to a paste. Beat this into the hummus.

Increase the oven temperature to 200°C/fan 180°C/Gas Mark 6 and bake the bread pieces for a few minutes until crisp and beginning to brown at the edges.

While the baguette pieces are still hot, spread thickly with the hummus and decorate with the reserved carrot and a few strips of pickled carrot and raisins lifted from the liquid.

Sprinkle the top with the spring onion and add a drizzle of olive oil, if you like.

TIP
To make your own hummus, see the Keen Cooks section, page 176.

Cream cheese, red onion & beetroot in a bagel

Beetroot and cream cheese is a marriage made in heaven. And it's particularly good in a crisp, hot bagel.

1 large red onion, sliced

1 tsp olive oil for frying

2 small, cooked beetroots

2 poppy seed bagels

100g cream cheese

drizzle of balsamic glaze

1 tbsp chopped chives

sea salt flakes and freshly ground black pepper

Fry the red onion gently in the oil until it is soft and beginning to brown.

Cut the beetroots into small dice.

Split the bagels horizontally and toast them.

Spread the bottom sides of the toasted bagels thickly with the cream cheese, then add the beetroots, cooked red onion, a drizzle of balsamic glaze and the chives. Sprinkle with salt and pepper.

Top with the bagel lids.

TIPS

Blue cheese or goat's cheese make good alternatives to cream cheese.

(v) To make it vegan, use vegan cream cheese.

Focaccia with grapes, fennel seeds & cottage cheese

This is simplicity itself, and there are few things nicer if the focaccia and cottage cheese are both very fresh. The grapes add a touch of sweetness, which works well with the anise flavour of the fennel seeds. No need to fry or roast the grapes if you are pressed for time. It just makes them slightly more interesting, especially if you eat them while the grapes are hot and the cottage cheese chilled.

1 tsp fennel seeds

20 large seedless red grapes

1 tsp olive oil for frying

2 good squares of focaccia

small tub of cottage cheese

sea salt flakes and freshly ground black pepper

Toast the fennel seeds in a dry pan, shaking them over the heat until you can smell them.

Turn the grapes in the oil, then fry them over a high heat until one of them bursts (4–6 minutes). Tip into a saucer.

Warm the focaccia squares by laying them in the hot pan for a minute or so. Then remove to 2 warm plates, spread them with the cottage cheese, season with salt and pepper and top with the grapes and fennel seeds.

TIP

(v) To make it vegan, use a vegan soft cheese, or hummus, instead of the cottage cheese.

English garden on crusty white

You can make this at any time of the year of course with good supermarket veg, but I especially like it in the spring when our first young veg appears in the garden. If you can get a big soft loaf so that each person has a large, not-too-thick slice of toast spread with curd cheese, it will make a delicious, unusual and substantial lunch. We are lucky enough to have a farmer's market selling fresh goat's curd, but any mild white spreadable cheese will do.

any spring baby vegetables such as:

  tiny carrots, with their fronds, if possible

  fresh young peas

  radishes

  asparagus spears

  baby beetroots

2 slices from the middle of a large white loaf

butter for spreading

150g goat's curd, ricotta, or any fresh mild white cheese

drizzle of olive oil (optional)

sea salt flakes and freshly ground black pepper

Prepare the veg: wash and dry everything. Don't bother to peel the carrots if they are very young, just halve them and leave a little of the stalk on them. Pod the peas (and leave a couple in their pods for interest, if you like). Trim the radishes and quarter some and finely slice others. Trim any woody stalks from the asparagus spears (see page 97).

Boil the asparagus and peas for no more than 2 minutes and rinse them under cold water. Boil the beetroots for 5–10 minutes, or until a sharp knife will penetrate them with only a little pressure. Quarter them, too, if you like.

Toast the bread. If the slices are too big for the toaster, brown them on both sides under the grill. Cool them, then spread with butter and the goat's curd.

Season with salt and pepper and arrange the veg on top.

Drizzle with a very thin stream of olive oil and scatter with carrot fronds, if you like.

TIP

(V) To make it vegan, use vegan butter and vegan cream cheese.

Classic bruschetta on artisan white bread

(V)

This simple Italian antipasto of raw chopped tomatoes on bread is only worth making in summer when the tomatoes are sweet and flavourful and, preferably, vine-ripened. For me, the delight of a good bruschetta is the contrast of crisp fried, even a bit charred, bread at the edge and the slightly soggy middle where the tomato juice has soaked in. Bruschetta is usually eaten as an appetiser with drinks, as in our photo. If this is lunch, you will need at least two each, as in this recipe.

4 slices of good white bread

olive oil for frying

1 large fat garlic clove

4–5 medium-sized ripe tomatoes, peeled (see tip, below)

a few squashy black olives, roughly chopped

Paint the bread slices with olive oil and brown them on a griddle pan or heavy frying pan, allowing them to char a little.

Peel the garlic clove and cut off the very end. Rub the clove, cut side down, gently all over one side of the toasts.

Cut the tomatoes into small cubes with a sharp knife and spread them over the bread. Sprinkle each slice with chopped black olives.

TIPS

- To peel tomatoes, cut a little slit in the skin of each one. Drop the tomatoes into boiling water and take the pan off the heat. In 10 seconds, if the tomatoes are ripe, the skins will have started to peel back where you made the slits. Drop the tomatoes into cold water to stop them cooking and then peel them. Unripe tomatoes will need longer in the hot water.

- If making bruschetta to eat with knife and fork, don't worry if the tomato topping wants to fall off the bread. But if it is to be a hand-held snack, chop the tomatoes small and don't pile them too high. Press them down with your hand to squash them into the bread a bit too.

- You could swap the tomato for avocado. Or, if serving with drinks, make a plateful of each.

Ricotta, tomato & sweet potato on wholemeal sourdough

Semi-dried tomatoes are a modern pleasure – much milder than the sometimes over-strong sundried ones, but concentrated and sweet nonetheless. You can find them in the deli section of large supermarkets.

1 medium sweet potato, peeled and cut into thin discs

130g semi-dried tomatoes in oil

2 slices of wholemeal sourdough bread, toasted

100g ricotta

½ tsp chilli flakes

4 basil leaves, shredded or torn

sea salt flakes and freshly ground black pepper

Preheat the oven to 180°C/fan 160°C/Gas Mark 4.

Put the sweet potato discs, spread out, to one side of a baking tray. Dip a pastry brush into the oil from the tomatoes and brush them. Bake for 20–30 minutes.

When they are almost done, lift the tomatoes out of their oil (but keep the oil) and put them on the empty side of the baking tray. Bake for a further 5 minutes.

Spread the toast with the ricotta.

Put the tomatoes, sweet potato and the remaining oil from the tomatoes into a bowl and add the chilli flakes and basil. Season well with salt and pepper, mix gently, then pile on to the bread.

TIPS

If you didn't get enough oil with your semi-dried tomatoes to coat the tomatoes and sweet potatoes, use a little extra virgin olive oil or walnut oil instead.

Ⓥ To make it vegan, use vegan ricotta.

Lentils, fried onions & cherry tomatoes on flatbread

Don't be daunted by the long list of ingredients here. They are easy to get and really quick to prepare. The lentil mix is a version of the classic Lebanese homely dish *mujadara*, which was first introduced to me by my sister-in-law. I love it. It makes, with that other classic, tabbouleh, and with a few labneh cheese balls, the most satisfying and delicious lunch. I confess to using ready-cooked lentils for this recipe. I prefer the Merchant Gourmet brand that come in a packet rather than canned lentils, which are sometimes seriously overcooked. If you do cook your own, use green or brown lentils, not orange or yellow ones, which are too small and are better in soups.

150g cooked Puy lentils

½ large red onion, finely chopped

8 cherry tomatoes, halved

3 tbsp olive oil, plus extra for brushing

2 garlic cloves, crushed

pinch of chilli flakes (optional)

1 tbsp chopped parsley leaves

good pinch of dried thyme

1 tbsp chopped thyme leaves

1 tsp chopped mint leaves

2 fresh round flatbreads (for homemade, see page 178), or pitta breads

20g feta cheese, crumbled

salt and freshly ground black pepper

Mix the first 10 ingredients together, reserving 1 tsp chopped herbs for the top. Season the mix with salt and pepper.

Toast the breads lightly, then brush them with olive oil. Pile the lentil mix on the breads and crumble the feta over the top, sprinkling with the reserved herbs.

TIP

Ⓥ To make it vegan, use vegan feta and flatbread.

Chunky guacamole & pine nuts on olive oil focaccia ⓥ

This is true luxury Bliss on Toast. And with the pine nuts and the olive oil in the focaccia, it is pretty rich. But it tastes light and healthy and is glamorous enough for a brunch or lunch party.

1 tbsp pine nuts

1 large avocado

5 ripe cherry tomatoes

1 small garlic clove

squeeze of lemon juice

1 tbsp olive oil

2 squares of focaccia

leaves from 2 basil sprigs

salt and freshly ground black pepper

Toast the pine nuts by shaking them in a dry frying pan over a high heat until they begin to brown. Tip them on to a cold saucer to prevent them from over-cooking. Or toast them in a microwave for 4 minutes, giving them a stir halfway through.

Cut the avocado flesh into cubes.

Halve the tomatoes and crush the garlic.

Gently mix the avocado, tomatoes, garlic, lemon juice and olive oil together and season with salt and pepper.

Pile on to the focaccia and top with the basil leaves and pine nuts.

TIP

If making this in advance, rinse the cubes of avocado under cold water. I don't know why, but I swear this delays them going brown in the air.

Pastes & spreads on crispbread

Spreading pastes on crispbreads or fingers of toast is so common-or-garden that I hesitated to include something quite so ordinary. But then, they are delicious and leaving them out just because they are simple to do seems daft in a book that aims to make life easy. Anyway, I can't resist, so here are a few suggestions (not all vegetarian or vegan I'm afraid, which I trust you will forgive; I thought it simpler to group them all here). Why not do a selection either for tea, or a TV supper or a picnic?

tapenade with watercress ⓥ

peanut butter with crab apple jelly ⓥ

anchovy paste with grapes

cream cheese with Marmite (ⓥ to make it vegan, use vegan cream cheese)

salmon pâté with tarragon leaves

chicken liver pâté with mint jelly

duck pâté with candied citrus peel

ricotta with pesto

Asparagus with hollandaise on white sourdough

I love hollandaise sauce, because it turns almost anything into a treat: broccoli, beans, mangetout and lightly cooked courgettes are delicious coated in it. So are poached eggs of course and all grilled fish. Happily (because hollandaise is a bit of a faff to make) you can buy it in a jar. Look for one that is made with the proper ingredients: eggs, butter, vinegar, salt and pepper. And little else!

250g asparagus spears

2 large slices of white sourdough bread

olive oil for griddling

3 heaped tbsp store-bought hollandaise sauce (or see tip, below)

1–2 tbsp milk

salt

Break a spear of asparagus in half, then cut the rest of the spears to match the length of this one, discarding the tough ends. Bring a frying pan of water to the boil and add 1 tsp salt. Cook the asparagus in this for 4–8 minutes depending on their thickness (they are done when a skewer or knife tip will penetrate the stalk with only a little resistance). Drain, then pat dry on a clean tea towel.

Brush the sourdough slices with olive oil and brown them in a frying pan. Divide the asparagus between the toasts.

Preheat the grill. Thin the hollandaise to pouring consistency with a little milk and pour over the asparagus. Place under the grill until pale brown. Take care not to over-grill them, because if you do the hollandaise will curdle.

TIPS

If you want to make your own hollandaise, I've explained 2 methods (one made by hand and the other in a blender) in the Keen Cooks section (see page 174).

(V) To make it vegan, use store-bought vegan hollandaise and plant-based milk.

Fish

Smörgåsbord open sandwich on pumpernickel

A classic Scandinavian open sarnie. It could be part of a smörgåsbord! The first time I heard the word was in the early 1960s, when caterers at Chichester Festival Theatre served nothing but smörgåsbord to the audience before the show and at the interval. In those days of grim and lifeless public catering in England, it was a very welcome revelation.

1 medium egg

100g frozen, cooked prawns, defrosted

60g cream cheese

2 slices of pumpernickel or dark rye bread

10 thin slices of cucumber

2 large round red radishes, thinly sliced

squeeze of lemon juice

1 tbsp chopped dill

sea salt flakes and freshly ground black pepper

Boil the egg for 8 minutes, cool it under cold water, then peel and slice it.

Pat the defrosted prawns dry with kitchen paper.

Spread the cream cheese on the pumpernickel and arrange the cucumber, radish and egg slices over the bread. Top with the prawns. Sprinkle them with lemon juice, dill, a pinch of salt and a few turns of the pepper mill.

Smoked mackerel, tarragon & horseradish on rye

Smoked fish is perfection with anything creamy and bland. I've used all sorts of smoked fish with slices of mozzarella, clotted cream, cream cheese, goat's cheese, or ricotta, on toast, in sarnies or for canapés. What makes these special is plenty of tarragon and a tiny touch of horseradish.

1 tsp horseradish cream

2 tbsp crème fraîche

leaves from 2 large tarragon sprigs

2 slices of soft white rye bread

100g smoked mackerel

Beat the horseradish into the crème fraîche with half the tarragon leaves.

Toast the bread lightly and, when cool, spread with the crème fraîche mixture.

Pile the smoked mackerel (minus the skin) on the toast, then scatter the rest of the tarragon leaves on top.

TIP

If you like a squeeze of lemon juice with your smoked fish, it's a good idea to cut off the 2 ends of the lemon wedge so that the diner can get a firm grip to squeeze it, and also to remove the ridge of pith along the inside edge of the wedge (the bit that was the core of the whole fruit). This will mean you can remove any seeds and that the juice won't be deflected into the squeezer's eye!

White crab with Parmesan & radish on rye

Freshly picked and cooked white crab meat can be ordered online. It is also available frozen and in cans. I buy mine online from a fishmonger in Salcombe. He picks and freezes the crab on day one and it's delivered in little boxes on day two. It defrosts really fast (just drop the packet or box into room-temperature water for 30 minutes). I like it, as here, on seeded dark rye.

2 slices of rye bread

150g white crab meat

100ml mayonnaise

juice of ½ lemon

1 tbsp finely grated Parmesan cheese

a few Gem lettuce leaves

2 big round red radishes, finely sliced

sea salt flakes and freshly ground black pepper

Toast the bread, or not, as you prefer.

Mix together the crab, mayo, lemon juice and Parmesan.

Put the lettuce leaves on the bread, add the crab mix and scatter over the sliced radishes. Sprinkle with a very little salt and a twist or so of the pepper mill.

TIP
My husband prefers dark crab meat to the more expensive white flesh. He likes the heavier, crabbier flavour. If you do too, add some dark meat to the mix, or spread it on the toast before adding the lettuce. It's generally available online too, though not often in supermarkets.

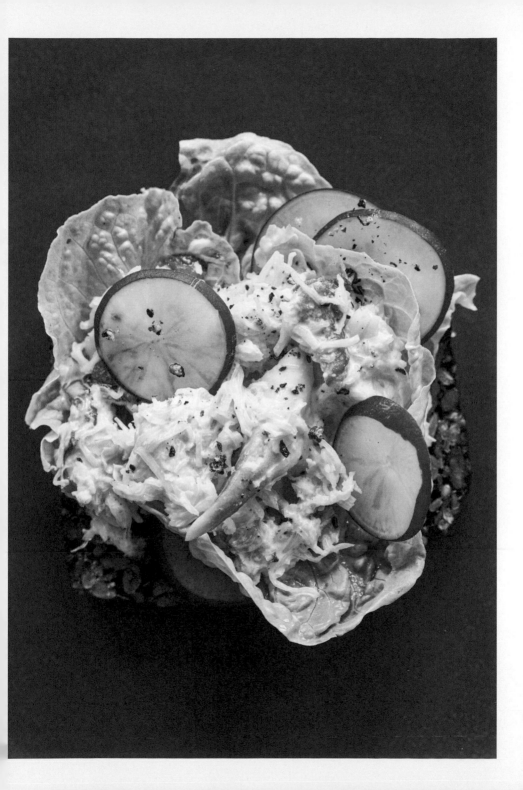

Mussels with samphire in bread 'bowls'

This is a hearty, absolutely delicious dish. The sauce soaks into the bread, but the sides remain crisp. My local supermarket sells cooked mussels in packets in the chilled cabinet. You can buy them online, too. Just avoid canned mussels, which are pickled.

a rectangular brown sandwich loaf

100g fresh samphire

1 garlic clove, chopped

1 small onion, finely chopped

small glass of white wine or cider

150ml double cream

200g cooked mussels, defrosted if frozen

sea salt flakes and freshly ground black pepper

Preheat the oven to 160°C/fan 140°C/Gas Mark 3.

Start with the bread. Cut a 2cm slice off each end of it. Scoop out a little of the soft middle of these slices so that you have 2 shallow bread 'bowls'. Put these into the oven until they are browning round the edges and are crisp and a bit dried out.

Now for the samphire. Discard any woody or tough stalks. Rinse well to get rid of some of the salt (it grows on the sea-washed shore) and then boil for 4 minutes in unsalted water. Drain, then rinse under the cold tap to 'set' the colour. (All green veg tends to lose its brilliant green if kept hot for long.) Dry on kitchen paper or a clean tea towel.

Now the mussels. Put the garlic, onion and wine or cider in a saucepan and boil down until the liquid has all but evaporated. Add the cream and boil again. Then add the mussels, immediately turn off the heat and cover the pan.

When ready to serve, put the bread squares, crust sides down, on dinner plates.

Add the samphire to the mussel pan and season with salt and pepper. Reheat briefly, then spoon (sauce and all) into and over the bread squares. Serve at once, while the bread is still crisp.

Asian-style prawns & asparagus on wholemeal

Large prawns always seem like a huge treat to me. And so does asparagus, so this recipe is right up my street. I think the big prawns tend to have more flavour than the little pink ones served in prawn cocktails, or bought ready-cooked and frozen.

2 slices of wholemeal farmhouse loaf

10 asparagus spears

3 tbsp mayonnaise

6 cooked tiger prawns, shelled (see tip, below)

¼ medium red chilli, deseeded and finely chopped

2 tsp freshly grated ginger

1 tbsp chopped coriander leaves

½ tsp coriander seeds, lightly crushed

juice of 1 small lemon

salt and freshly ground black pepper

Toast the bread slices.

Cut the woody ends off the asparagus (see tip, below) and boil the spears in salted water until just tender (about 4 minutes). Cool under cold water, then drain and pat dry.

Spread the mayonnaise thickly on the toast. Lay the asparagus spears on top.

Mix the cooked prawns with the chilli, ginger, coriander leaves and seeds, lemon juice and a little salt and pepper. Divide the prawns between the 2 toasts.

TIPS

- To know where to cut asparagus stalks, take one of the spears and use your hands to break it in half. The point where it breaks is the place to cut: below that will be tough and stringy, above it tender.

- If cooking your own prawns rather than buying them ready-to-eat, see the Keen Cooks section, page 177.

- The easiest way to grate ginger is when it's frozen. I always keep mine in the freezer firstly because, while frozen, it grates, skin and all, to a fine dust very quickly and cleanly, and secondly because it keeps for ever and doesn't shrivel up as it does in the fridge.

Tuna Niçoise baguette

I think the best Niçoise salad is made with fresh tuna. When raw (or raw inside and cooked outside, as here) the flesh is silky-smooth, delicate tasting and dark red. Once cooked through it is exactly like canned tuna or the filling of a tuna sandwich, with a distinctive strong flavour, flaky texture and opaque pink colour. Potato is a traditional ingredient of a Niçoise, but I have replaced it here with the baguette 'boats'.

250g fresh tuna, in 1 evenly thick steak

2 tbsp olive oil, plus more for frying and brushing

30cm piece from the middle of a baguette

50g French beans

2 tsp red wine vinegar

1 garlic clove, crushed

Gem lettuce

5 cherry tomatoes, halved

a few thin slices of red onion

1 anchovy fillet, chopped (optional)

2 hard-boiled eggs, quartered

a few black olives

2 basil sprigs

salt and freshly ground black pepper

Get a non-stick frying pan (preferably a ridged griddle, to create stripes) piping hot. Brush one side of the tuna steak with olive oil and put it oil side down into the hot pan. Don't turn it for least 30 seconds, until brown on the underside. Then turn it over to brown the other side (you are aiming for brown outside and still-raw middle). Allow to cool.

Preheat the oven to 200°C/fan 180°C/Gas Mark 6. Split the length of baguette in half. Pull out a little of the crumb inside to hollow out the bread pieces. Brush the inside generously with olive oil and bake in the hot oven to crisp and begin to brown. Allow to cool.

Top and tail the beans and drop them into boiling water for 4 minutes, then drain and rinse them in cold water. Dry on kitchen paper.

Mix the 2 tbsp olive oil with the vinegar and garlic and season well with salt and pepper.

Break the lettuce into separate leaves and lay the leaves inside the bread 'boats', then divide the tomatoes, beans, onion slices, anchovy (if using) and eggs between them.

Slice the tuna neatly and add to the baguette halves. Spoon over the dressing and top with the olives and basil sprigs.

Old-fashioned anchovy toast fingers with pear pickle

This is the simplest and most irresistible snack. Because it is so delicious, I've reckoned on two rounds each. If you stack them as we have in the picture, they will stay crisp while you eat them. We used to have this in coffee bars and pubs when I was young in South Africa, but you hardly ever see anchovy toast now.

4 large slices of white sandwich bread

butter for spreading

about 2 tbsp anchovy paste

For the pickle

2 large ripe pears, peeled and diced

1 tbsp sugar

4 tbsp apple cider vinegar

4 tbsp water

½ tsp ground ginger

squeeze of lemon juice

Simmer the pickle ingredients together in a small pan with the lid on until tender (15–30 minutes, depending on the ripeness of the pears). Allow to cool.

Toast the bread to a good dark brown. Spread it generously with butter, then sparingly with anchovy paste.

Cut each piece of toast into 4 fingers and divide between 2 plates. Serve with the pear pickle.

TIP

Anchovy paste is not that easy to find, though large supermarkets sometimes stock it in tubes. You can still get a very strong version of it as Gentleman's Relish in large supermarkets and you can buy anchovy paste online. Or you could blitz canned anchovies to a paste in a blender.

Scallop Caesar on fried bread

The secret to any Caesar salad is getting the dressing right. So many pubs seem to think bottled mayo straight out of the jar will do. It's fine to use that as a base though, in which case omit the egg yolks and oil from the recipe below and add all the other ingredients to 2 heaped tbsp mayo. I've omitted croutons, as we are serving this on fried bread.

Many people don't like 'corals' – the orange part of a scallop. But as many, like me, love them, I'd suggest you leave them on.

1 Gem lettuce

6 fresh king scallops

oil and 2 tsp butter for frying

2 slices of white bloomer

1 tbsp olive oil for frying

handful of watercress or lamb's lettuce

salt and freshly ground black pepper

For the Caesar dressing

3 anchovy fillets from a can

1 garlic clove, crushed

½ tsp Dijon mustard

1 large egg yolk

1 tbsp finely grated Parmesan cheese

1 tbsp lemon juice

½ tsp freshly ground black pepper

2 tbsp olive oil

In a mortar or small blender, grind all the dressing ingredients except the oil to a paste, then beat in the oil, little by little. Now that's a Caesar dressing! Tear up the lettuce leaves and turn them in the dressing.

Cut away any hard white muscle attached to one side of the white part of the scallops. Wash in cold water and pat dry on kitchen paper.

Heat a couple of tbsp of oil in a frying pan and fry the 2 slices of bread to brown on both sides. Drain on kitchen paper, then put on separate plates. Pile the dressed salad on top.

Turn the scallops in the 1 tbsp olive oil. Reheat the pan until piping hot. Carefully lay the scallops in it and fry fast for 2–3 minutes (depending on size) without moving. (Shifting them about will stop them browning.) Turn and fry for another minute, adding the butter, a pinch of salt and a good grinding of pepper. Arrange 3 on top of each Caesar toast.

Tip any buttery pan juices on top and add the watercress or lamb's lettuce. Eat at once. The scallops should be barely cooked in the middle.

Smoked salmon, wasabi & avocado on granary bread

This is not on toast, but it *is* bliss. The texture is so decadently soft, it seemed a pity to spoil it with crunchy toast, so I have stuck to bread. I had something like this, made with home-cured gravlax, in a Michelin-starred restaurant. As gravlax (which is raw unsmoked salmon cured with salt, sugar and lots of dill) is not easy to find and takes at least two days to make, I thought bought smoked salmon would be easier. But if you can get gravlax (sometimes spelled gravadlax), give it a try. It's sweeter and milder.

2 tbsp fresh curd cheese
or cream cheese

1 tsp wasabi paste

2 slices of granary bread

1 ripe avocado

150g smoked salmon
or gravlax

finely grated zest of 1 lime

½ tsp each of black and
white sesame seeds

a few pea shoots or tendrils
(optional)

Mix the cheese with the wasabi and spread it on the bread.

Slice the avocado thinly and put it in an even layer on top of the wasabi-cheese mix, then cover with the smoked salmon.

Sprinkle on the lime zest and sesame seeds and garnish with the pea shoots or tendrils, if you have found any.

TIP

You can sometimes buy wasabi paste in tubes, but it's usually sold as dry powder and must be mixed to a paste with a little water.

Sardines, red onion & spinach on focaccia

Sardines on toast, a frequent Sunday night supper of my parents, was never a great favourite of mine, but this version is delicious. The onion and lemon counter the oiliness of canned sardines, and the richness of the fish is nicely balanced by the focaccia. Give it a go. I think you'll love it.

small packet of baby spinach leaves

1 can of sardines in oil

2 squares of focaccia

¼ red onion, thinly sliced

squeeze of lemon juice

sea salt flakes and freshly ground black pepper

First bring a saucepan half-filled with water to the boil and drop in the spinach leaves. Turn them gently with a wooden spoon until wilted and then drain. Dunk briefly in cold water to 'set' the bright green colour, drain again, then spread on a tea towel and pat dry.

Carefully lift the sardines out of their oil.

Put the focaccia squares on separate plates and use some of the sardine oil to paint their tops. Then spread the spinach on top of them and dab it with more of the sardine oil.

Divide the sardines between the plates and top with the onion slices. Squeeze lemon juice over them and sprinkle with salt and pepper.

TIP
This works well with canned marinated mackerel fillets, too.

Potted shrimps with pickled fennel on wholemeal toast

I used to think potted shrimps the height of luxury. Smart restaurants in the 1970s would send them out in their little pots and ceremoniously upend them on to your hot toast. They are still a great treat. They are traditionally made with the tiny, flavourful Morecambe Bay brown shrimps, cooked and set in butter flavoured with a touch of nutmeg and cayenne. They are sold in one-serving pots. Because there is plenty of butter in the pot, I don't butter the toast. The shrimps can be served cold, with the butter still set hard, or warm, with it melted. I like it, as here, halfway between the two. I also like a pickle with them, but this is hardly essential. A lemon segment will do fine.

2 thick slices of wholemeal bread

2 jars or tubs of potted shrimps, defrosted if frozen

a few rocket leaves

For the pickled fennel

handful of thin slices of raw fennel

50ml apple cider vinegar

50ml water

½ tsp coriander seeds, lightly crushed

To make the pickle: in a small saucepan, bring the fennel slices, vinegar, measured water and coriander seeds to the boil. Simmer for 2 minutes, then allow to cool.

Toast the bread well and put it on plates.

When ready to eat, put the shrimp pots into the microwave for 20 seconds or so until the butter is half-melted. Then turn them out on to the toast and sprinkle with the fennel, lifted out of its pickling liquid, and the rocket.

TIP

These fennel-pickling quantities are just for this recipe. But it might be worth scaling them up and pickling a whole fennel bulb, finely sliced. It will keep in its liquid in the fridge for weeks.

Tuna & sweetcorn toastie

This is a hugely popular combination, and rightly so. Cooked-through or canned tuna is miles away from raw or just-seared fresh tuna, but it is delicious and children generally love it. Over the years I have written recipes for tuna and sweetcorn bake, pie, pancakes, pizza and pasta. And no one needs a recipe for a tuna and sweetcorn sandwich, but here's how to make the perfect fried parcel.

80g canned tuna

60g canned sweetcorn

30g grated Cheddar cheese

4 large slices of very fresh white sandwich bread

1 tbsp each butter and oil for frying

salt and freshly ground black pepper

Break up the tuna with a fork and mix it with the sweetcorn and Cheddar. Add salt and pepper to taste.

Cut the crusts off the bread and spread the tuna mix on 2 of the slices, leaving a 1cm margin round the edge uncovered. Use the remaining bread slices to cover the tuna, pressing the edges together to seal the sandwiches.

Melt the butter and oil in a frying pan over a medium heat and, when hot, add the sandwiches. Leave them alone until the first side is brown, then carefully turn them to brown the second side.

TIPS

- This old-fashioned British fried sarnie method is a simpler, less sophisticated version of the Italian Mozzarella in Carrozza (see page 32). There is more danger of the filling spilling out of the edges of the sandwiches, so don't be tempted to over-fill them.

- This sort of fried toastie can be used to stretch all sorts of leftovers into another meal: Bolognese sauce, ratatouille, any kind of stew, curry or casserole. Anything that will go in a pancake or pie will go in a fried toastie – even sweet things such as banana and chocolate spread, or stewed apricot and apple, though they, I think, need a jug of custard too.

Dublin Bay prawn cocktail on seeded brown toast

My idea of heaven is unlimited numbers of Dublin Bay prawns (otherwise known as langoustine or scampi). I once had supper with the Laird of North Uist, Earl Granville, who had been catching them that day. We sat round the table with an enormous cauldron in front of us, overflowing with steaming prawns just out of the pot, and a few hours before that, out of the sea. They were huge, like little lobsters, and I've never tasted anything like them – nor made such a pig of myself. Had there been any left over, this is what I'd have made for lunch next day.

2 slices of seeded brown bread

butter for spreading

½ small Gem lettuce, shredded

150g ready-cooked and peeled Dublin Bay prawns

1 small ripe avocado, sliced

¼ red onion, finely chopped

For the Marie Rose sauce

2 tbsp mayonnaise

1 tsp tomato ketchup

squeeze of lemon juice

1 tbsp chopped parsley and tarragon leaves

salt and freshly ground black pepper

To make the sauce, mix the mayo and ketchup together and season to taste with the lemon juice, salt and pepper and only half the herbs.

Toast the bread lightly, and when cold, butter it and pile the shredded lettuce on top.

Mix the sauce gently with the cooked Dublin Bay prawns, avocado and onion. Pile the mixture on top of the lettuce. Sprinkle with the rest of the herbs.

TIP

If you have bought your prawns raw and still in their shells, you will need to cook them. See the Keen Cooks section, page 177.

Meat & Poultry

Chicken tikka with yogurt on naan

Chicken tikka has long been one of the UK's most loved flavours and makes a great sandwich, pitta or wrap filling. But this is what it was born for – to eat with hot naan or chapati.

100ml plain yogurt

juice of ½ lemon

1 tbsp tikka paste

4 raw skinless and boneless chicken thighs

oil for the tray

2 small naans, or chapatis

butter for spreading

½ mild red chilli, finely chopped

a few mint or coriander leaves (or both)

sea salt flakes and freshly ground black pepper

Preheat the oven to 240°C/fan 220°C/Gas Mark 9.

Mix the yogurt, lemon juice and tikka paste together and reserve half of it for later. Turn the chicken thighs in the rest and spread them out on an oiled baking tray. Roast for about 35 minutes until brown and cooked through (a skewer should glide through the flesh easily). Slice each thigh into 3.

Warm the naans or chapatis briefly in the microwave or toaster and spread with butter.

Pile the chicken on to the breads, seasoning with a little salt and pepper. Top with a dollop of the reserved yogurt, the chilli and herbs.

TIP
Bone-in or boneless? Most packs of chicken thighs come either with skin on and bone in, or skinless and boneless, which is certainly the easiest and quickest to deal with. If you can't get them like this, get them on the bone and remove the skin, then use a small sharp knife to cut and scrape the flesh from the raw thighbones. Don't be tempted to cook them first, because if you remove the skin and bones after cooking, half the flavour will go with them.

Peking duck with pomegranate, on a soft roll

One seldom has leftover duck, but I sometimes buy a whole duck and roast it for the two of us, we eat the breasts, then I shred the legs for this. Hoisin sauce and roast duck is a marriage made in heaven, and the spring onion and cucumber cut through the richness.

200g well-done roast duck (or see tip, below)

1 tbsp hoisin sauce

2 soft white hotdog rolls

butter

small Cos or large Gem lettuce leaves

5cm piece of cucumber

2 spring onions

1 tbsp pomegranate seeds

salt and freshly ground black pepper

Shred the cooked duck, discarding any skin and fat. Mix it with the hoisin sauce and add salt and pepper to taste.

Cutting from the side, split the soft rolls just enough to open them like a half-open book. Butter the inside of each roll and push a few lettuce leaves into each.

Cut the cucumber into thin sticks, leaving the skin on. Remove roots and outer leaves from the spring onions and shred into long strips. Divide these and the cucumber sticks between the rolls with the lettuce. Top with the duck and pomegranate seeds.

TIP

If wanting a shortcut, many supermarkets sell portions of roast duck, ready to reheat and shred. They may come in kits including pancakes and hoisin sauce and so on. Or you can buy confit of duck in a jar: expensive, but so worth it! As the duck is cooked and preserved in fat, you will have to remove the fat and skin before shredding the meat.

Englishman's treat on soft white bread

These classic English flavours are unbeatable. A thick slice of fresh bloomer, a generous dollop of mustardy mayonnaise, some not-too-salty ham, a few capers and a sprinkling of parsley make a substantial lunch-time snack for the seriously hungry.

1 tsp English mustard

100ml mayonnaise

2 thick slices of bloomer or any soft bread

200g cooked ham (see tip, below)

1 tsp rinsed and dried capers

1 tbsp chopped parsley leaves

Mix the mustard and mayo together and spread it thickly on the bread.

Chop the ham into chunks (or if already in slices, shred it). Mix the ham with the capers and parsley and pile it on to the bread.

TIP
I prefer to boil my own ham. I get 1kg of 'green' (non-smoked) raw ham hock from the butcher and cook it very slowly. I use it in thick slices for a main meal with a poached egg on top, then in thin slices for salads, and finally I use the misshapen knuckly bits of ham for this.

New York sourdough slice

Hard-boiled eggs and salt beef; a very old-fashioned combo, but so good! Spread liberally with mustardy mayonnaise and with the kick of pickled cucumber, this combination should satisfy the hungriest troops.

2 slices of sourdough bread, preferably seeded

100ml mayonnaise

2 tsp wholegrain mustard

2 good slices of salt beef or pastrami

2 hard-boiled eggs, peeled and chopped

1 large dill pickle (sweet, pickled cucumber), chopped

1 tbsp chopped parsley leaves

Toast the sourdough, if you like.

Mix the mayo with the mustard and spread the sourdough with half of it. Then lay the slices of salt beef or pastrami on top.

Mix the eggs, pickled cucumber and the rest of the mayonnaise mixture together and use this to top the beef. Sprinkle with the parsley.

TIP

I prefer the large, mild pickled cucumbers (dill pickles) which are both sweet and sour. But you may prefer the small, sharper little gherkins, in which case you will need 3–4 of them, and you should chop them finely.

Roast lamb with gremolata on fried ciabatta

If you've had roast lamb for Sunday lunch, this is the perfect Sunday night supper. Make the gremolata first. It will keep for a few days in the fridge and leftovers will make a great salad dressing.

2 slices of ciabatta

olive oil for frying

100g cold sliced roast lamb

For the gremolata

small cup of parsley leaves (no stalks)

1 large garlic clove, crushed

finely grated zest of ½ lemon and a few julienned strips to serve

1 tsp lemon juice

75ml olive oil

pinch of chilli flakes

salt and freshly ground black pepper

To make the gremolata, put all the ingredients in a food processor or blender, season, and chop to a rough paste.

Brush the ciabatta on both sides with olive oil and cook in a frying pan, turning to brown both sides.

Lay the roast lamb slices on the ciabatta, spoon the gremolata on top and sprinkle with the lemon zest julienne.

TIP

I like warm toast and cold roast lamb, but if you prefer your lamb warm, heat the slices briefly in the pan when the bread is done.

Fried prosciutto, watermelon & feta on Melba toast

This surprising combination is remarkably good. I thought of wrapping chilled watermelon in hot prosciutto for a challenge on a TV programme when I was asked to produce something delicious out of the 'watery tasteless waste of space that is the watermelon.' I didn't agree with the diagnosis and I'm glad to say I succeeded in persuading watermelon's critics of its virtues.

2 thin slices of white bread

1 big fat (2cm wide) slice from the middle of a watermelon

a little vegetable oil

4 slices of prosciutto or Parma ham

1 tbsp toasted pine nuts (see tip, below)

50g crumbled feta cheese

squeeze of lemon juice

1 tbsp chopped mint leaves

drizzle of balsamic glaze

1 tbsp pomegranate seeds

Toast the bread, trim the crusts and allow to cool. Now, put them back in the toaster repeatedly for very short bursts to dry them out without burning, aiming for crisp rusks.

Peel the watermelon, then cut 4 even-as-possible rectangular blocks (7 x 2 x 2cm) of watermelon flesh. Don't worry about any pips.

Get a frying pan good and hot with a thin coating of oil. Wrap a slice of prosciutto round each block of melon and fry, seam down, in the pan. Prosciutto cooks fast: stand over it and carefully turn the blocks to brown on all sides.

As they are done, lift 2 on to each piece of toast. Then sprinkle with the pine nuts, feta, lemon juice and mint. Lastly add a drizzle of balsamic glaze and a scattering of pomegranate seeds.

TIPS

- I sometimes serve this for a dinner party starter, with the crisp bread on the side.
- Nuts burn in a flash. The easiest way to toast them is to give them bursts in a microwave: first for 2 minutes, then stir, then cook for 1 minute at a time. Pine nuts take about 4 minutes. Or stand over them as you shake them in a dry frying pan.
- As a general rule of thumb, the darker the flesh of a watermelon, the sweeter its taste.

Asian turkey salad on thick white toast

This combo makes an unusual lunch out of leftover turkey. Thai fish sauce (*nam pla*) is a great standby for adding a burst of flavour to almost anything, especially salads and fish or poultry dishes. Of course, Cambodians and Thais wouldn't eat this on toast, but it makes a perfect lunch.

butter for spreading

2 thick slices from a white batch loaf, toasted

1 tbsp cashew nuts

200g cooked turkey, shredded

2 spring onions, chopped

½ tsp finely chopped chilli

1 tbsp chopped coriander, plus a few sprigs

2 tbsp Asian fish sauce (nam pla)

1 tbsp caster sugar

2 tbsp lime juice

2 tsp lemon grass paste

Butter the toast.

Toast the cashew nuts in a dry pan, shaking them over a medium heat until beginning to colour. Or toast them in the microwave for 5 minutes, stirring them halfway through.

Combine all the other ingredients in a bowl and turn gently to mix. Pile on to the toasts and top with the coriander sprigs and cashews.

TIPS

- This is good hot, too. Gently heat the turkey mix in a frying pan or the microwave. Make the toast at the last minute and top it with the hot turkey.

- I keep tubes or jars of pastes in the fridge, because you often only need a tiny amount and it's not worth crushing lemon grass (very laborious!) or chopping a chilli for a minute flick of it. I have garlic, lemon grass, coriander, chilli, ginger and harissa pastes in shop-bought tubes.

Spanish beans on fried bread

This is a LOT more interesting and delicious than beans-on-toast! It's the perfect speedy supper for the family, or a late-night snack that even non-cooking teenagers could manage. An artisan baker's white bloomer loaf would be best for this, but to be honest, any thick white loaf will do.

oil for frying

2 thick slices of white bread

80g sliced chorizo

½ tsp smoked paprika

6 ripe cherry tomatoes

400g can of white (cannellini) beans

1 tbsp chopped parsley leaves, plus a few whole leaves

Put a splash of oil into a large frying pan, swirl it round to coat the surface, then fry the bread slices in the pan, turning to brown both sides.

When well browned, take the bread out and put in the chorizo slices, smoked paprika and the cherry tomatoes, with 1 tbsp more oil if necessary.

Fry, shaking the pan occasionally, until the tomatoes are softened and the chorizo is beginning to brown.

Drain the beans, add them to the pan and simmer all together until hot. Stir in the chopped parsley.

Serve on the toast, with, just for the sake of appearances, a few parsley leaves on top.

Jubilee chicken with mango & avocado on ciabatta

The mildly curried Coronation (or Elizabeth) chicken was invented by the Cordon Bleu cookery school for a diplomatic lunch held at Lancaster House after Queen Elizabeth's coronation. It has been a British staple ever since, the recipe serving as a festive buffet dish or a humble sandwich filling. But since June 2022 was The Queen's Platinum Jubilee, I thought that a bit of a reset might be in order. The original had apricot jam in it, which I've replaced with hot mango chutney, while a bit of fresh mango cuts the richness, I think. I've also added some avocado.

1 tbsp strong curry paste

200ml mayonnaise

juice of ½ lemon

250g cooked chicken, free of skin and bones

½ mango, peeled, stoned and cut in chunks

2 spring onions, chopped

1 tbsp hot mango chutney

½ avocado, peeled and sliced

2 slices of ciabatta, toasted

1 tbsp chopped coriander

Stir the curry paste into the mayonnaise, add the lemon juice and then thin the sauce down with water until it is just liquid enough to coat the back of a spoon.

Mix half the sauce with the chicken, mango, spring onions and mango chutney.

Lay the avocado slices on the toast and pile the chicken mixture on top of it. Use the rest of the mayo to drizzle over the chicken and add a sprinkling of coriander.

TIP

The original Coronation chicken was deliberately mild, to cope with 1950s nervousness about 'foreign food'. My version is a bit punchier, but of course you can regulate the flavour by adding only 1 tsp curry paste to the mayonnaise to begin with and increasing it until it suits your tastebuds.

Triple-decker ham & cheese brown bread sarnie

This is the perfect satisfying lunch for hungry folk after a walk in the snow, or a spell of standing in the cold on a touchline. Any cheese you like will make a great sarnie, but I like Emmental or Gruyère, conveniently bought in pre-sliced packets. It's such a simple assembly it hardly needs a recipe, but I would advise preparing and assembling all the ingredients before you make the toast, so it's still warm when eaten.

8 slices of thin brown sandwich bread

butter for spreading

4 slices of Emmental or Gruyère cheese

2 thick slices of ham

small packet of watercress

1 tomato, thinly sliced

2 tsp piccalilli

Toast all the bread slices and butter them.

Put 2 slices of cheese each on 2 slices of toast. Now put the ham on another 2 slices, the watercress and tomato on a further 2 slices and spread the piccalilli on the final 2.

Stack them up: cheese, then ham, then veg and finally the piccalilli slice – turned upside down – on top.

TIP
If you want to cut your sandwiches in half, which will look nicer, stick a cocktail stick through each half of the sandwich to keep the layers from sliding.

Bayonne ham & burrata on toasted croissant

When I was 19 and working in south-west France, near Bayonne, as an au pair, I had my first slice of the region's unsmoked, dried raw ham. And ever since I've fancied it superior to all other *prosciutti crudi*. I'm sure if I'd been working for an Italian family in Parma, I'd be singing the praises of Parma ham. But those early gastronomic memories stay with you, don't they? That job introduced me to cassoulet and gateau Basque too and I still make them both.

1 burrata cheese, at room temperature

2 large plain croissants

4 slices of Bayonne ham, or prosciutto

Drain the burrata of its whey and pat it dry in a clean tea towel or on kitchen paper. Divide the cheese into 2 equal halves.

Use a serrated knife to slice the croissants in half horizontally. Toast them, or heat in a medium oven (preheated to 180°C/fan 160°C/Gas Mark 4) for about 6 minutes.

Immediately after the croissants emerge from the toaster or oven, lay first the ham and then the cheese on the 2 bottom halves and put the top halves in place. If not ready to eat at once, put them back in the oven for up to 5 minutes to warm up.

TIP

If the croissants are soft and limp (it is surprising how many shopkeepers will put your baked goods in a plastic bag, guaranteeing they'll lose their crispness), don't despair. Just heat them slowly in a warm oven (preheated to 160°C/Fan 140°C/Gas Mark 3) before splitting them.

Peppered steak & salsa verde on sourdough toast

A good steak sandwich has got to be one of life's purest pleasures. And this version is my favourite. The old-fashioned peppered coating is as delicious as it was in the 1970s, while the simple salsa verde is the perfect sharp accompaniment to the rich, buttery meat.

2 tbsp black peppercorns, coarsely crushed

2 thin sirloin steaks, fat removed

oil and butter for frying (see tip, below)

2 slices of sourdough bread

For the salsa verde

1 tbsp each chopped tarragon, parsley and mint leaves and chives

½ tbsp chopped gherkins

½ tbsp capers

1 tbsp wine vinegar

½ tsp Dijon mustard

100ml extra virgin olive oil

First make the salsa verde by combining all the ingredients.

Warm 3 plates.

Press the peppercorns into the flesh of the steaks on both sides. Fry the steaks in the oil and butter, carefully turning them once.

When done (see tip, below) put them on a warm plate to rest for a few minutes while you toast the bread slices and spread the toasts with a layer of salsa verde.

Put the toasts on to the remaining warm plates. Slice the steaks and add to the toasts.

TIPS

- To cook the perfect steak, heat 1 tsp each oil and butter in a heavy frying pan. Dry any moisture off it with kitchen paper. Put it into the hot pan and press it down with a spatula. Then leave it for at least 2 minutes. Don't be tempted to move it until you see drops of moisture rising to the surface. When you do, flip it and brown the other side. A 'blue' steak will feel very soft (like raw meat) when you push it with a finger. At rare, it will still be soft but not positively squashy; at medium it will be more resistant but still pliant; at well-done it will feel hard.

- Oil or butter? I use both for frying steak because the butter adds flavour while oil, having a higher burning point, allows you to heat the pan to the good frying heat that you need.

Japanese chicken with katsu curry sauce on white toast

In the last century, the European habit of breadcrumbing food before frying caught on in Japan, where it evolved into the fashionable katsu with panko crumbs, replacing the flour-egg-and-breadcrumbs of the West. In Japan, katsu is served with a sauce, sometimes curried. In recent years we have returned the compliment and katsu is now widely eaten; the sauce comes in sachets from the supermarket.

cupful of panko breadcrumbs

1 tbsp cornflour

4 tbsp water

1 packet of raw chicken mini fillets, or 1 large raw chicken breast, cut into strips

2 spring onions

½ small mild fresh chilli

2 thick slices of white bread

butter for spreading

3–4 tbsp store-bought katsu curry sauce (or see tip, below)

oil for frying

handful of rocket

Tip the breadcrumbs into a shallow bowl. Mix the cornflour with the measured water in a second shallow bowl and turn the chicken pieces first in this, then in the breadcrumbs, making sure they are all completely coated.

Trim the roots and outer leaves from the spring onions, then cut them into 2.5cm-long pieces on the diagonal. Slice the chilli (discarding the seeds if you don't like it hot).

Toast the bread, butter it and put each slice on a plate.

Warm the katsu sauce in a pan or microwave, according to the packet instructions.

Pour 2–3 tbsp oil into a frying pan and heat until a breadcrumb will sizzle in it. Fry the chicken fillets for a few minutes on each side until brown.

Put the rocket on top of the toasts and add the chicken pieces. Blob katsu curry sauce over them and top with the spring onions and chilli.

TIP

If you want to make katsu sauce from scratch, it's very easy and you'll find the recipe in the Keen Cooks section (see page 174).

Black pudding & apple on brown baguette

Black pudding's strong flavour is not everyone's cup of tea, but it's certainly mine. I think my Scottish husband would divorce me if I didn't like black puddin' and haggis. I love them both, but black pudding in the traditional Scottish breakfast fry-up is just perfect. And it's mighty good on toast too.

12cm piece from the middle of a brown baguette

butter for spreading and frying

1 dessert apple

1 tsp caster sugar

4 slices of black pudding, each about 1.5cm thick

4 small young sage leaves

Split the piece of baguette in half. Remove a little of the soft crumb from the 2 pieces to hollow them out a little, then spread them with butter and put them into a hot oven (preheated to 200°C/fan 180°C/Gas Mark 6) to crisp up. When they are beginning to brown at the edges, turn the oven off and open the door briefly to cool it down.

Meanwhile, peel the apple and cut it into 8 segments. Sprinkle with the sugar and fry in a little butter until softened and beginning to caramelise. Then put the segments on a saucer in the still-warm oven.

Remove the plastic-y wrapping from the slices of black pudding and fry them in the same pan, adding more butter if needed and turning them over so both sides are fried to a darker brown. Fry the sage leaves too, until crisp.

Fill the baguette halves with the apple and black pudding and top with the sage leaves.

TIP

I buy a whole black pudding online and then cut it into 5cm pieces which I freeze. I extract these for suppers-for-2, or for deepening the flavour of dishes made of minced meat, such as shepherd's pie, meatballs or Bolognese sauce, crumbling a few slices of black pudding into the mix. It works wonders.

Student heaven on thick white toast

Baked beans carry a heap of baggage, don't they? Everyone is very firm about how they like them best, or 'the only way' to eat them. I like them with salad and French dressing. My husband cannot abide them hot. One friend will only eat them straight from the can – a hangover from student days. Many swear the gold standard is Heinz and all other brands are pale imitations. The most popular way to eat beans is, of course, on toast. Here's a slightly souped-up version.

2 chipolata sausages

40g smoked bacon lardons

2 tsp oil for frying

400g can of Heinz baked beans

2 thick slices of white bread, toasted

butter for spreading

handful of rocket or watercress (optional)

Twist each of the chipolatas in the middle until they each become 2 cocktail sausages.

Fry the lardons in the oil, tossing them frequently in the pan to brown them all over. Lift them out when done and put the sausages into the fat in the pan. Fry slowly, rolling them to brown them evenly all over. They are done when they feel firm, no longer squashy.

Return the lardons to the pan, add the beans and warm through.

Toast and butter the bread and pile the beans on top. Serve with the rocket or watercress on the side, if you like.

TIPS

- You can buy smoked lardons in supermarkets, but occasionally you can only get the smoked fatty bacon in rashers, not mini-cubes or 'lardons'. If so, cut them across into little strips.
- Fried onion, slices of spicy or smoked sausage, a crumbled slice of black pudding, a fried egg or grated cheese all turn baked beans into more of a treat. If you are vegan, squares of tofu or Quorn, seasoned with paprika and black pepper, make a good addition.

Fried chicken livers & grapes on focaccia

I'll tell anyone who'll listen that liver is delicious, but it seems the habit of eating offal might die out with my generation. I find the shudders at the thought of tongue or kidneys inexplicable. Why do we happily eat the backside of a pig, but not its liver? It's mad. But some 20-year-olds will happily eat pâté, or a terrine, made of liver, so I live in hope of an offal comeback.

2 squares or slices of focaccia

40g butter for spreading and frying

1 tsp Dijon mustard

200g tub of chicken livers

100g large red or black seedless grapes, halved

80ml double cream

sea salt flakes and freshly ground black pepper

Toast the bread lightly. (If the focaccia is too thick to go in your toaster, you can warm the pieces in a frying pan or under the grill.) Spread them with a little of the butter and with all the mustard. Put them on warm plates.

In a large frying pan, heat the rest of the butter until just sizzling but not brown, tip in the livers and shake them to distribute them evenly. Leave them for a minute or so to brown on one side, then turn them over with tongs, one by one, to brown the other sides. You are aiming to cook them until pink inside, not dark purple, which they are when still raw. (Cut one open and have a peek.) Tip them into a bowl and keep them warm (covering them with a folded tea towel will do it).

Quickly fry the grapes in the same pan you used for the livers, tossing them until good and hot, then tip them into the bowl with the livers.

Use a slotted spoon to lift the livers and grapes on to the mustardy toast. Pour any juices from the liver bowl into the hot frying pan and pour in the cream. Swirl it about until it bubbles, then immediately pour it over the livers and grapes. Sprinkle with salt and pepper.

Gammon & pineapple (its good, really!) on walnut bread

In the 1960s, a round of canned pineapple placed on top of a slice of gammon (ham from the leg) – sometimes with a glacé cherry in the middle and sprinkled with brown sugar – grilled until brown and bubbly, was first considered the height of sophistication, then later the depth of ignorant vulgarity. I don't think I ever made such a thing, but during lockdown, for want of other ingredients, I gave it a go. Well, sort of. And the result is delicious, I promise.

2 × 1cm-thick raw gammon steaks

2 slices of walnut bread, toasted

For the pineapple salsa

150g fresh pineapple, finely chopped

1 tbsp mango chutney

squeeze of lemon juice

1 tsp chopped parsley leaves

½ tsp finely chopped red chilli

First make the salsa by combining the ingredients.

Preheat the grill to maximum.

Grill one side of the steaks for 3 minutes to part-cook them. Turn them over and pile on the salsa, levelling the top.

Grill until the pineapple is just beginning to brown, by which time the gammon should feel firm rather than squashy. Lift on to the toast.

TIP
When buying ham, try to get good thick slices. Pre-sliced ham tends to be too thin and is generally already cooked. A butcher will cut you a couple of thick raw gammon steaks. Pre-cooked ham slices are fine for ham-and-eggs, but not suitable for this.

German cheese & sausage on rye

This recipe is a classic example of 'what grows together, goes together': German sausages are better, I think, with German mustard, pickled cabbage, rye bread and German-style cheeses such as Gouda, Emmental and Tilsit. Of course, this recipe would be good with English mustard, Cheddar, fresh cabbage and white bread... but maybe not quite *as* good. It's worth hunting down the authentic ingredients.

2 fresh bratwurst sausages

oil for frying

2 slices of rye bread from a large loaf

2 slices of Tilsit or Emmental cheese

2 tbsp bottled or canned sauerkraut

mild German or 'hotdog' mustard

Fry the bratwurst in the oil over a medium heat; not too high or the tender skin of the wurst will split. Brown them all over for about 10 minutes. Remove to a plate.

Meanwhile, toast the bread, put the slices on warm plates and, while hot from the toaster, add a slice of cheese to each piece.

Drain the sauerkraut and dry it on kitchen paper.

Tip the sauerkraut into the hot sausage pan and shake over the heat until steaming hot, then spread it over the cheese-topped bread and lay the hot sausages on top.

Drizzle mustard zig-zag fashion all over the top.

TIPS
- I buy mild mustard in a squeezy plastic bottle, which makes drizzling a doddle. If your mustard is in a jar, no matter, blobs will do as well as zig-zags.
- If you don't have sauerkraut, you can make instant pickled cabbage: the recipe is in the Keen Cooks section (see page 175).

Bacon butty with avocado & green pepper relish

When, years ago, I was on the British Rail board, I had a letter from a customer complaining that, on the Midland line, she couldn't get the excellent bacon butty she'd enjoyed on the Great Western. I investigated and found we didn't sell bacon butties anywhere, but one enterprising steward on the GWR had spotted a gap in the market and was bringing in his own ingredients to exploit it. The British do love a bacon butty, and this is a deluxe unbeatable one.

1 small or ½ large avocado

6 rindless, air-dried, thinly sliced streaky bacon rashers, or pancetta strips

2 large white baps

butter for spreading

For the relish

¼ green pepper

¼ red apple, cored

¼ medium-hot red chilli

2 tsp balsamic glaze

squeeze of lemon juice

To make the relish, chop the green pepper very small, excluding the seeds. Don't peel the apple, just chop it to match the green pepper. Chop the chilli as finely as you can. Mix all the relish ingredients together.

Slice the avocado.

Preheat the grill and grill the bacon until crisp and evenly brown all over.

Split the baps, butter them and brown the buttered sides under the grill. Spread the bottom halves with the relish, then add the bacon and finally the avocado. Put on the tops.

TIP
If making these for a brunch party, it might be wise to offer the relish separately. There are purists about who'd shudder at adulterating the famous bacon butty with abominations such as pepper relish…

Fillet steak with Café de Paris butter on brioche

No one knows for sure what the original recipe for the famous Café de Paris butter for steak was but, honestly, whatever you leave out from this long list, it won't matter. Any or all of it tastes great. The essentials, in my book, are the butter (obviously) and the mustard, onion, curry, parsley and orange zest.

2 small fillet steaks

butter and oil for frying

2 thick slices of brioche

For the Café de Paris butter

60g butter, soft but not melted

1 tsp capers, finely chopped

1 tsp finely chopped shallots or onion

1 tsp each of Dijon mustard, tomato ketchup and curry paste

1 tsp each of chopped parsley and tarragon leaves, dill and chives

finely grated zest of 1 small orange and 1 lemon

pinch of salt

For the Café de Paris butter, beat everything together, spoon the mixture on to a piece of clingfilm or beeswax wrap and shape it into a fat patty shape. Chill it, then cut the patty into 2 rounds.

Dry any moisture from the steaks with kitchen paper. Melt 1 tsp each of butter and oil in a medium-hot frying pan. When the butter starts to sizzle, put in the steaks and don't touch them until you see beads of moisture forming on the upper sides (3–4 minutes). Then turn them over and brown the other side for another 2 minutes or so. When the steaks feel as you want them (see page 138), put them on a warm plate and cover.

While the steaks are resting for a few minutes, toast the brioche.

Then put the steaks (and any juices) on the brioche and top with a round of Café de Paris butter.

TIP

I can't eat steak without a bit of salad. How about a few watercress or rocket sprigs? Both have that touch of bitterness which cuts the richness of steak and butter.

Desserts

Baked apple with mincemeat on a teacake

Most of my misshapen and scabby apples from the garden go into jelly, which I foist on to friends. But I save some medium-sized good-looking apples for old-fashioned baking. I stuff them with mincemeat, which is more interesting than traditional raisins.

2 dessert apples

1½ tbsp ground almonds

1½ tbsp mincemeat

knob of butter, melted

1 tbsp caster sugar

2 tbsp crème fraîche

1 tbsp brandy

1 large teacake

icing sugar for dusting

Preheat the oven to 160°C/fan 140°C/Gas Mark 3.

Use an apple corer to remove the apple cores. Score a line through the skin of the 'equator' of each (to stop the apples bursting in the oven) and put them in a small lined roasting tin.

Mix the ground almonds into the mincemeat and stuff the centre holes of the apples with this.

Brush with butter and sprinkle with half the sugar. Bake until a skewer will glide easily right through an apple (about 40 minutes).

Meanwhile mix the crème fraîche, the rest of the caster sugar and all the brandy together.

Split the teacake horizontally to make 2 thinner discs and toast them.

Serve the hot apples on the teacake halves with the cream and sift over icing sugar.

TIPS

- Any dessert apple will do, but I think Granny Smiths are the best for this. They are crisp, tart and keep their shape. Cooking apples are generally too large, cook to a soft purée and will need more sugar; delicious, but too messy.
- You may wonder what the ground almonds are for. They are there to soak up the juices and stop escaping syrup from burning in the oven.
- (v) To make it vegan, use margarine instead of butter, vegan mincemeat and brandy, and replace the crème fraîche with unsweetened smooth coconut yogurt.

Greek yogurt, mixed berries & honey on a waffle

This is the quickest and most satisfying pud, or a weekend breakfast treat. Canned or frozen (and defrosted) berries, or cut up and pitted apricots, peaches or plums, stewed apples or rhubarb, all work well too. The trick is a good runny honey and nice fresh waffles.

2 shop-bought waffles (or see tip, below)

50ml runny honey

100g mixed berries (defrosted if frozen)

100g Greek yogurt

Warm the waffles in a toaster.

Carefully spoon the honey all over the waffles, then add the fruit (without too much of the juice if it was frozen) and top with the yogurt.

TIP

If you would like to make your own waffles, the recipe for them is in the Keen Cooks section (see page 181). Be warned though, you will be at it for ages, doing second helpings for everyone.

Apricots, almonds & clotted cream on an English muffin

This is the most divine, indulgent and irresistible pud. Don't skimp on the cream or jam. Better forgo it altogether than try to make it healthy! It's best made with ripe fresh apricots. If using canned fruit, roast them anyway – it will deepen their flavour.

2 large apricots,
or 3 small ones

40g butter, half of it melted

2 tsp caster sugar

1 English muffin,
split and toasted

2 tbsp apricot jam

1 tbsp flaked almonds,
toasted (see tip, below)

1 small pot of clotted cream

Get the grill as hot as possible.

Halve the apricots, remove the stones and put the halves, stoned side up, on a grill tray. Brush them with the melted butter and sprinkle with the sugar.

Grill, not too close to the elements or gas flame, for 8–10 minutes until brown round the edges.

Meanwhile, butter the toasted muffin halves and put them on warm plates. Spread them with apricot jam and share the apricot halves between them.

Sprinkle with the almonds and serve with clotted cream.

TIP

You can toast the flaked almonds in the oven under the grill tray at the same time as roasting the apricots, but they burn in a flash, so be careful. Safer, probably, to stand over them while you gently turn them in a frying pan, or toast for 3 minutes in the microwave, giving them a stir halfway.

Fried Christmas pudding, brandy cream & blackberries

This is hardly Bliss on Toast, since the pudding stands in for the toast and it is the star of the show. But I could not resist including it: fried Christmas pud is a such a wicked Boxing Day treat. I like it even better than the first time around. The sugar tends to caramelise a bit in the frying pan and the edges of the pudding become toffee-like and delicious.

3 tbsp double cream

pinch of mixed spice

1 tbsp brandy

butter for frying

2 evenly thick slices of Christmas pudding

caster sugar for dusting

6–8 blackberries (canned are fine), halved if you like

First make the spiced cream: whip the cream until it is thick enough to hold its shape, then flavour it with the spice and brandy.

Melt a good blob of butter in a heavy frying pan. Dust the slices of pudding in sugar and fry on both sides in the butter.

Serve hot with a good dollop of the cream and a few blackberries on top.

TIPS

- If using canned blackberries, which is all that is likely to be around in December, lift them from the can with a slotted spoon and drain them on kitchen paper.
- Easy alternatives to blackberries are canned mandarin segments, or fresh clementines, peeled and sliced across into rings.
- (V) To make it vegan, be sure the pudding and brandy is vegan, and that you use oil for frying and a vegan whipping cream for the topping.

Bostock with rum & coconut yogurt

I'd never heard of Bostock until I discovered, a few years ago, that it was *the* fashionable thing in New York. Basically, it was invented by French bakers to make use of leftover brioche. Leftover brioche is unheard of in my house, but it's worth making or buying extra just to make this. And no, I've no idea why it is called Bostock, and neither has Google!

4 thick slices of brioche

1 tbsp smooth raspberry jam

1 tbsp flaked almonds

icing sugar for dusting

100ml smooth coconut yogurt, unsweetened

1 tbsp rum

1 tsp runny honey

For the frangipane

30g ground almonds

drop of almond extract

1 egg, lightly beaten

15g caster sugar

15g room-temperature butter

Preheat the oven to 200°C/fan 180°C/ Gas Mark 6.

Beat together the frangipane ingredients.

Spread the brioche slices with the jam and then the frangipane. Sprinkle with the almonds.

Bake in the oven for 12–14 minutes until the almonds are just beginning to colour. Remove and sift a little icing sugar over the tops.

Mix the yogurt, rum and honey together and serve on the Bostock, warm from the oven.

TIPS
- All sorts of variations are possible. I like to use apricot jam, add chopped dried apricots to the frangipane and serve the Bostock warm with crème fraîche. Stem ginger in the topping cream is good too, as is ground cinnamon.
- This works well with leftover Christmas panettone, too.
- This is so delicious you might like to make double quantities and eat them for breakfast next day.
- (v) To make it vegan, use vegan block instead of butter, vegan brioche, rum and vegan egg, and replace the honey with maple syrup.

Bananas & ice cream with brandy syrup on panettone

I first had this in a pub in the Cotswolds years ago. I've been trying ever since to recapture it exactly, without success. But this is close, and divine. Not the healthiest of puds, with all that butter. I just remind myself that Fernand Point, the great French chef of the 1930s, believed the secret of cuisine was butter. He said 'Give me butter! Always butter!' He'd be hung, drawn and quartered today, but, once in a while, a bit of indulgence is good for you, no?

butter for frying

1 tbsp blanched (skin off) hazelnuts

2 thick slices of panettone

2 bananas

2 tbsp golden syrup

1 tbsp brandy

2 balls of best vanilla ice cream

Now for a lot of frying in butter. Keep the frying pan at medium heat to prevent the butter burning. Melt a little butter and fry the nuts briefly to brown, then tip on to a cold saucer to stop them burning. Melt 1 tbsp more butter and brown the panettone on both sides, adding more butter if needed. Lift on to warm plates.

Peel and split the bananas lengthways. Fry the halves in more butter, flat sides down, just to get them nicely brown on those sides. Place them browned sides up on the panettone slices.

Mix the golden syrup with the brandy.

Scoop a large ball of ice cream for each plate and place on the panettone. Sprinkle with the nuts and pour over the brandy syrup.

TIP

If you can't get blanched hazelnuts, here's how to get the skins off. Toast them in a microwave: cook them in a single layer for 3 minutes, then stir and give them a few 1-minute blasts, checking after each, until the skins crack and they start to brown. Or toast in a dry pan, shaking it to get the skins hot and blistering. Or bake in an oven preheated to 200°C/fan 180°C/Gas Mark 6 for 10–12 minutes. Rub in a tea towel to remove the skins. Whatever you do, watch them. Nuts burn in a moment.

Keen Cooks

When writing *Bliss on Toast*, I kept wanting to include recipes for making ingredients from scratch, then having to remind myself that I'd promised to keep it simple and use store-bought ready-mades if they were good. And since we can now get a wealth of excellent pre-prepped things in supermarkets, I have stuck to my resolution. But sometimes one doesn't have the store-bought answer and the homemade-from-scratch ingredients are at hand in the kitchen cupboard. So I have signalled – in the tips beneath the recipes – when I've included instructions for the do-it-yourself version, which you will find in the pages that follow.

Hollandaise sauce

To make hollandaise by hand

Put 2 large egg yolks and 1 tsp white wine vinegar into a small heatproof bowl set over (but not touching) just-simmering water. Whisk as you slowly add, drip by drip, 150g melted butter. The sauce will gradually thicken. Season with salt, pepper and lemon juice.

To make hollandaise in a blender

Blitz 2 large egg yolks and 1 tsp white wine vinegar together, slowly pouring in 150g melted butter in a thin stream while the machine is running. Season with salt, pepper and lemon juice. If you curdle the hollandaise (which you won't if you pour slowly), there is nothing for it but to start again with another egg yolk and gradually add the curdled mixture to it, beating all the time.

Tomato sauce

Chop 1 large onion and fry it in olive oil until soft and yellowish. Add a couple of crushed garlic cloves (or a squeeze from a garlic tube). Cook for 1 minute, then add a 400g can of tomatoes – and any slightly manky tomatoes you want to get rid of, chopped up – and a dollop of tomato paste or purée. Simmer for 20 minutes or so. Taste and season with salt and pepper, and maybe, if it is too sour, 1 tsp sugar.

Katsu curry sauce

Chop up 1 large onion, 1 large carrot and 1 dessert apple. Fry them with 1 crushed garlic clove in a little oil. When soft, add 1 tsp curry powder, ½ tsp ground ginger, ½ tsp ground turmeric and a 400g can of coconut milk. Bring to the boil and simmer, stirring occasionally, until thick.

Quick Pickling

Nasturtium 'capers'   ⓥ

If you grow nasturtiums, the flowers are pretty (and delicious) in salads and you can quick-pickle the seedpods (called berries for some reason). I prefer them to capers, which can be a bit vinegary. For a cupful of seedpods, bring a small pan of 100ml apple cider vinegar, 100ml water, 1 tbsp sugar, 10 peppercorns and ½ tsp coriander seeds to the boil. Pour over the seedpods in a heatproof bowl and leave to cool. They will keep in the liquid for weeks in the fridge.

Instant pickled cabbage   ⓥ

Finely shred ¼ white cabbage and pack into a clean jar. Bring to the boil 300ml water and 300ml white wine vinegar with 1 tbsp sugar, 1 tsp caraway seeds and ½ tsp salt. Pour over the cabbage, pressing the cabbage down to sink it. Allow to cool, then store in the fridge, where it will keep happily for 2–3 weeks. (If pickling thick cabbage stalks, boil them briefly in the pickling liquid before cooling.)

Hummus

To make hummus from scratch ⓥ

Process together the chickpeas from a 400g can, 1 garlic clove, 1 small mild chilli, a good squeeze of lemon juice, 60ml tahini and 60ml olive oil. Beat until smooth and creamy. Season with salt and pepper.

Red pepper hummus ⓥ

Process together the chickpeas from a 400g can, 2 roasted red peppers from a jar (or 2 home-roasted peppers), 1 crushed garlic clove, 1 small mild chilli, a good squeeze of lemon juice, 2 tbsp tahini and 60ml olive oil. Blitz until smooth and season with salt and pepper.

Cooking prawns from scratch

If your prawns are grey, they are raw. They go pink on cooking. To cook raw prawns still in the shell, fresh or frozen, just drop them into salted simmering water and wait a few minutes until they are just pink. Drain them at once and rinse them in cold water to stop them cooking further. All prawns and shrimps become hard and rubbery if overcooked. Shell them by pulling off tails and heads and splitting the skin down the belly to remove it.

If you have bought them raw and shelled, fry them briefly in a little oil until just pink, then tip them on to a cold plate to cool.

Flatbreads

This is the easiest of bread doughs, and very satisfying to make. You just mix equal quantities of self-raising flour and Greek yogurt together (120g of each for 2 breads, 360g of each for 6) with a pinch of salt. Draw the mix into a ball and knead for a few seconds until you have a smooth, soft dough. If it's too dry and stiff, add more yogurt or a splash of water. If too sloppy (this all depends on the quality of the flour) then add more flour. Divide the dough into the same amount of pieces that you want breads. Use a little oil to grease a rolling pin and a work surface. If your flatbread is to have a topping and will be eaten with knife and fork, roll each piece out into the size of a saucer. If it is to be a wrap, roll until thin and about the size of a dinner plate. Get a griddle or heavy frying pan really hot and cook the flatbreads to brown them, for a minute or so on each side. To keep them warm until eating, wrap them in a tea towel.

If serving flatbread by itself, or with a curry, I like to brush it with butter and crushed garlic while it is still hot; sometimes I add chopped herbs and/or chopped mild chilli.

wholemeal

olive bread

flatbread

english muffin

wholemeal sourdough

naan

baguette

bloomer

seeded sourdough

pain de campagne

walnut

olive sourdough

granary

poppy seed bagel

chilli

Waffles

Make a batter by blitzing together 150g self-raising flour, ½ tsp baking powder, 1 tsp sugar, 2 medium eggs, and 240ml milk. Cook the batter in a waffle maker according to the manufacturer's instructions. (In essence: heat it, brush the inside with melted butter, fill one side with the batter, close the lid, cook until steaming and smelling delicious. Open up. If it's brown, it's done.) In the absence of a waffle maker, you could just make thickish pancakes with the batter: pour a little batter slowly into an oiled hot frying pan. When it has spread to the diameter you want your pancake to be, stop pouring and let it cook until it is bubbly on top and set and brown underneath. Turn over to cook the other side. Repeat until all the batter has gone. I like them American-style, topped with crisp bacon and maple syrup, for breakfast.

rye 50% dark 50% light

brown baguette

hotdog roll

pitta

light rye

oat

pumpernickel

ciabatta

seeded wholemeal

teacake

soft white rye

focaccia

brioche

sourdough

soft white bap

grilled courgettes with cashew pesto on rye 48
red pepper hummus, avocado & zhoug on rye 65
smoked mackerel, tarragon & horseradish on rye 90
white crab with Parmesan & radish on rye 92

S

salads: Asian turkey salad on thick white toast 128
  spicy ezme salad with fried egg on country loaf 16
salmon: smoked salmon, wasabi & avocado on granary bread 104
salsa, pineapple 148
salsa verde: peppered steak & salsa verde on sourdough toast 138
salt beef: New York sourdough slice 122
samphire: mussels with samphire in bread 'bowls' 94
sandwiches: bacon butty with avocado & green pepper relish 152
  smörgåsbord open sandwich on pumpernickel 89
  triple-decker ham & cheese brown bread sarnie 134
sardines, red onion & spinach on focaccia 106
sauces: hollandaise sauce 174
  katsu curry sauce 174
  tomato sauce 174
sausages: German cheese & sausage on rye 151
  student heaven on thick white toast 144
scallop Caesar on fried bread 103
scrambles with fried prosciutto on sourdough 30
shallots: tomatoes, shallots & oregano on black olive toast 60
shrimps: potted shrimps with pickled fennel on wholemeal toast 109
smoked mackerel, tarragon & horseradish on rye 90
smoked salmon, wasabi & avocado on granary bread 104
smörgåsbord open sandwich on pumpernickel 89
sourdough: asparagus with hollandaise on 84
  avocado, summer tomatoes & tapenade on olive 54
  kale, chilli, burrata & tapenade on 36
  New York slice 122

peppered steak & salsa verde on toast 138
ricotta, tomato & sweet potato on wholemeal 77
scrambles with fried prosciutto on 30
summer peas & beans with ricotta on 21
Tenderstem broccoli & egg with romesco on 18
Spanish beans, fried bread 130
spicy ezme salad with fried egg on country loaf 16
spinach: goat's cheese, spinach & red onion 35
  sardines, red onion & spinach on focaccia 106
student heaven on thick white toast 144
summer peas & beans with ricotta on sourdough 21
sweet potatoes: ricotta, tomato & sweet potato on wholemeal sourdough 77
sweetcorn: tuna & sweetcorn toastie 110

T

tapenade: avocado, summer tomatoes & tapenade on olive bread 54
  kale, chilli, burrata & tapenade on sourdough 36
teacake, baked apple with mincemeat on a 159
Tenderstem broccoli & egg with romesco on sourdough 18
toastie, tuna & sweetcorn 110
tomatoes: avocado, tomatoes & tapenade on olive bread 54
  chunky guacamole & pine nuts on olive oil focaccia 81
  classic bruschetta on artisan white bread 74
  lentils, fried onions & cherry tomatoes on flatbread 78
  ricotta, tomato & sweet potato on wholemeal sourdough 77
  Spanish beans on fried bread 130
  Tenderstem broccoli & egg with romesco on sourdough 18
  tomato sauce 174
  tomatoes, shallots & oregano on black olive toast 60
  tomatoes with English pesto on toasted focaccia 45
triple-decker ham & cheese brown bread sarnie 134
tuna Niçoise baguette 98

tuna: tuna & sweetcorn toastie 110
  tuna Niçoise baguette 98
turkey: Asian turkey salad on thick white toast 128

V

vegetables: English garden on crusty white 72
  see also individual types of vegetable

W

waffles 181
  Greek yogurt, mixed berries & honey on a waffle 160
walnut bread, gammon & pineapple (it's good, really!) on 148
wasabi: smoked salmon, wasabi & avocado on granary bread 104
watermelon: fried prosciutto, watermelon & feta on Melba toast 127
Welsh rarebit with crisp bacon on granary 14

Y

yogurt: chicken tikka with yogurt on naan 117
  Greek yogurt, mixed berries & honey on a waffle 160

Z

zhoug: red pepper hummus, avocado & zhoug on rye 65

Store Cupboard

Miscellaneous

Brandy

Cooked Puy lentils in a sachet

Oils: rapeseed oil, extra virgin olive oil, olive oil, truffle oil

Panko breadcrumbs

Raisins

Rum

White wine or cider

White wine vinegar, red wine vinegar, apple cider vinegar

Spices

Black peppercorns

Chilli flakes

Coriander seeds

Dried thyme

Ground cardamom

Ground cinnamon

Ground cumin

Ground ginger

Mixed spice

Sea salt flakes

Smoked paprika

Sumac

Wasabi

Nuts & seeds

Black and white sesame seeds

Blanched hazelnuts

Cashew nuts

Fennel seeds

Flaked almonds

Ground almonds

Pine nuts

Pumpkin seeds

Walnuts

Sauces & pastes

Anchovy paste (in a tube)

Chilli paste (in a tube)

Fish sauce (nam pla)

Garlic paste (in a tube)

Hoisin sauce

Hollandaise sauce

Horseradish cream

Katsu curry sauce

Lemon grass paste (in a tube)

Mayonnaise

Rose harissa paste

Strong curry paste

Sweet chilli sauce

Tikka paste

Tomato ketchup

Tomato purée

Tomato sauce

Jams & preserves

Apricot jam

Black olives /
squashy black olives

Black olive tapenade

Capers

Dill pickles

Gherkins

Hot mango chutney

Marmite

Mincemeat

Peanut butter

Piccalilli

Raspberry jam

Red onion marmalade

Runny honey

Sundried tomatoes /
semi-dried tomatoes
in oil

Flavourings

Almond extract

Balsamic glaze

Date syrup

Dijon mustard

Golden syrup

Mild German or
'hotdog' mustard

Pomegranate molasses

Raisins

Wholegrain mustard

Canned goods

Anchovy fillets

Cannellini beans

Confit of duck

Heinz baked beans

Mackerel fillets

Sardines in oil

Sauerkraut

Sweetcorn kernels

Tuna

Chilled goods

Garlic

Eggs

Lemons

Milk

Plain yogurt, Greek
yogurt, coconut yogurt

Frozen goods

Cooked mussels

Dublin Bay prawns
(aka langoustines
or scampi)

Ginger (frozen whole,
unpeeled, unwrapped)

King scallops, raw

Mixed peas, edamame,
broad beans

Potted shrimps

Sliced black pudding

Sliced prosciutto

Tiger prawns, cooked
and shelled

White crab meat

Dame Prue Leith, DBE, DL

Prue is probably best known for her role as a judge on 'The Great British Bake Off', but she has also been a judge on 'The Great British Menu' and 'My Kitchen Rules'.

She has published eight novels, a memoir (*I'll Try Anything Once*) and 14 cookbooks. Her recent cookbook, *The Vegetarian Kitchen*, which she co-wrote with her niece Peta Leith, was published in 2020.

Prue Leith's career has included her own restaurants, catering and cookery school businesses; she's been a board director of companies such as British Rail, Halifax, Safeway, Whitbread, Woolworths, and Belmond (ex-Orient Express) Hotels.

Prue has had a deep involvement with education and the arts: she chaired the first of the companies charged with turning round failing state schools and was Chair of the School Food Trust, responsible for the improvement of school food and food education. She started and led the campaign for contemporary sculpture to be exhibited on the Fourth Plinth in Trafalgar Square, London. She has been active in many charities and is the Chancellor of Queen Margaret University, Edinburgh. She was an advisor for the Government's Hospital Food Review.

Among her awards she has a DBE, 12 honorary degrees or fellowships from UK universities, the Veuve Clicquot Businesswoman of the Year award, and her restaurant, Leith's, won a Michelin star.

She is married with two children and four grandchildren.